# RURAL INDEBTEDNESS OF WEAKER SECTIONS IN TELANGANA

# RURAL INDEBTEDNESS OF WEAKER SECTIONS IN TELANGANA

Dr. D. Satyanarayana

AUTHORSPRESS

Worldwide Circulation through Authorspress Global Network
**First Published in 2019**
**by**
**Authorspress**
Q-2A Hauz Khas Enclave, New Delhi-110 016 (India)
Phone: (0) 9818049852
E-mail: authorspressgroup@gmail.com
Website: www.authorspressbooks.com

**Rural Indebtedness of Weaker Sections in Telangana**
**ISBN 978-81-942721-1-3**



Printed in India at Kensington Press

# Foreword

I feel it was a great honor to write foreword to the book entitled *Rural Indebtedness of Weaker Sections in Telangana.*

Agriculture plays a key role in the overall economic and social well-being of our country. The farmers who provide food and nutrition to the entire people in the nation. They also provide livelihood to millions of people in the country. Since the days of Green Revolution, our farmers have been used varieties of improved seeds and various sources of irrigation for their crops for the mass production. Hence the level of food production has increased but their agriculture income has decreased. The farmers can be classified as marginal, small and big farmers. Now-a-days the segmentation of small and marginal farmer's level has been increased due to partition of their properties. The small land holdings of farmers would increase the cost of cultivation. The sources of income of the farmers are, income from cultivation, wages for working in land, cattle rearing etc. The income of the farmers are not constant because their agricultural operation mostly depends on uncontrollable factors such an monsoon, climatic conditions, availability of labour, market price trend, etc.,

Hence, the inadequate income in agriculture would affect the majority of farmers living condition. Hence, it is forced them to get loan from money lenders at high interest rate he meet their day-to-day expenses. The all India rural credit survey committee clearly stated that Indian farmers born in debts, living in debts and die in debt. It is true and it continuous till now.

The burden of debt passes on from is generation to another generation. The number of those in the grip of this victitious problem is even now very large, despite vigorous attempts to solve it. Rural indebtedness has taken into the very vitals of our rural social structure. However, the problem of indebtedness depends upon the amount, nature and purpose of the loan taken. The commission agents come out to be the largest contributor towards loans in all the categories. They provided loans for productive as well as unproductive purposes.

Individual indebtedness becomes nation indebtedness, it is a continuous like chain. The statistics shows that the inflation is decreased, per capital income has earned increased and ultimately the economic growth of the nation is good. But in practical sense, the economic status of people in the rural area still in bad conditions. This is happiness due inadequate income of weaker sections. In this juncture, is essential to study the weaker sections financial status which would cure various economic diseases and it paves ways real individual and the nation growth. The book written by Dr. Dasari Satyanarayana, certainly throws light on to many issues involved in the study of rural indebtedness. These aspects focused by the author undoubtedly are helpful for research scholars, civil society and policy makers to evolve much more positive approach towards implications of rural indebtedness among weaker sections in the Telangana for the development of agriculture.

**Prof. A. Vinayak Reddy**
Former Registrar, Satavahana University
Karimnagar,
Telangana,
India

# Preface

This book *Rural Indebtedness of Weaker Section in Telangana* analyses the chronic melody that has been effecting the very vitals of the rural community, especially, the farming community. The weaker sections SC, ST and BC farmers suffer more as their land holdings are marginal and small. Non-farm employment opportunities and income generation activities are meager in the rural setup. Expansion of institutional agencies of credit has been spectacular both in volume and diffusion. But these sections hover around the non-institutional sources, particularly, money lenders for their credit needs unmindful of the consequences weaker sections of the rural areas comprising marginal and small farmers, artisans and land less labourers groan under the growing burden of the debt. These sections are highly inaccessible to the institutional credit in view of their poverty, near zero level asset base, ignorance and illiteracy. But these vulnerable sections have to invest more on production, marketing and consumption in the light of the rising inflation amidst the changes in and around the economy under the thrust of globalisation and the resultant techno changes. Consumption patterns, basket of goods, investment costs and inputs, nature and cost of child education, health expenditure and of every item of personal, social and economic life of the rural societies has under gone radical change and overall expenditure have shown upward movements. Incomes from agricultural produce are uncertain as the produce and the market prices are always uncertain. These sections are driven by compulsion to depend on the money lenders and private financial agencies, MFIs and middle men. They bear the brunt of the debt burden and remain helpless in the debt trap, live in the debt trap and leave the families in the slush of debt. Implications of indebtedness and stories of misery are untold in different parts of the country. Suicide attempts, suicides, social unrest, health problems, crop holidays are all on the increase and demanding the attention of the policy makers, academicians, civil society organisations.

In this context the present study attempts to explore the daunting problems of rural indebtedness from close corners in its depth by taking two adjoining districts i.e., Khammam and Warangal of the Telangana Region of Andhra Pradesh. Both the districts are included in the 31 districts identified for the Prime Ministers package of Rs. 100 crores. The study concentrates only on the weaker sections and analyses the inter-district and intra-district facets of the problem of the indebtedness.

After analysing the socio-economic conditions in the study area sources of the credit and credit flow are estimated. Caste category wise perception applied to identify the weaker sections for the analysis. Indebtedness is estimated in relation to land ownership, caste, asset and income levels and per household indebted quantum also been worked out. Utilisation of the credit purpose wise is examined. Implications of indebtedness from social, economic and personal points of view are examined.

The book is divided into six chapters based on various themes of the study. Chapter I deals with the introduction and methodology of the study. Chapter II presents the socio-Economic conditions of the study. Chapter III examines the utilisation of credit and implications of rural indebtedness. Chapter IV is devoted to the summary, conclusions and implications of the study.

This book is meant as a research for the researchers in economics and will be helpful for policy making towards welfare of farmers and agriculture development.

**Dr. D. Satyanarayana**

# Contents

# Acronyms

| | |
|---|---|
| APGVB | Andhra Pradesh Grameena Vikas Bank |
| BC | Backward Community |
| B.F. | Big Farmers |
| BPL | Below Poverty Line |
| GDP | Gross Domestic Product |
| IC | Institutional Credit |
| Km | Kilometers |
| M.F. | Marginal Farmers |
| Med.F. | Medium farmers |
| MFIs | Microfinance Institutions |
| NI | Net Income |
| NABARD | National Bank for Agricultural and Rural Development |
| NSSO | National Sample Survey Organisation |
| NGO | Non-Governmental Organisation |
| NIC | Non-Institutional Credit |
| PNB | Punjab National Bank |
| PACS | Primary Agricultural Co-operative Societies |
| RRBs | Regional Rural Banks |
| S.C. | Scheduled Caste |
| S.F. | Small Farmers |
| SHGs | Self-Help Groups |
| S.T. | Scheduled Tribes |

# 1

# Introduction and Methodology

"India lives in villages" said the father of the nation, Mahathma Gandhi. Yes, villages thrive on agriculture and agriculture is still the back bone of the Indian Economy despite concerted industrialisation and expansion of the service sector. In 1951 share of agriculture in the national income was 56.5 per cent. Over the years it has been decreasing and at present the share of agriculture 15.0 per cent in the national income. It implies that agriculture is still contributing in two digits to national income unlike in the developed countries like U.K. and U.S. in single digits. 59.0 per cent of the Indian population still depends on agriculture either cultivators or as agricultural labourers. Indian agriculture provides raw material to leading industries like Textile, Jute, Sugar, Vanaspathy and Plantation products. Small scale and cottage industries like Handloom weaving, Oil crushing depends on agriculture for raw material.

Food processing industry generates more income and employment. Agricultural products like Sugar, Tea, Oil seeds, Tobaco, Pulses constitute the main items of exports. Though in the recent years percentages of agricultural exports have been decreasing still they are around 10.0 per cent. Agriculture is the main support for transport system as movement of agricultural goods from place to place provide bulk of revenue to our transport system. Retail and whole sale trade with in the country is mostly in agricultural goods. Prosperity of agriculture in the rural areas provides market to the industrial goods. Most of the industrial goods derive demand from the country side as more than 70.0 per cent of the population live in villages. Failure of agriculture in any year creates several problems to the economy fall in demand for the industrial products. Agriculture provides food security and helps to eradicate poverty. It helps to contain raising prices and to increase employment and agricultural wages. Rural domestic savings from the farm households enable to augment resource mobilisation. Agriculture provides income to the government in the form of taxes at the different levels. For that matter, the very existence of Indian Economy depends on agriculture.

During the Plan period, under new strategy, in the form of Green revolution, the expansion of irrigation sources, mechanisation, application of chemical fertilizers and pesticides and changes in crop patterns have changed the nature of agriculture phenomenally. But Economic reforms since early 1990's caused crisis in agriculture. Planning Commission and Government are aware of the fact that growth rate of crop production and productivities have been declining.

The deceleration of the growth rate is very much disturbing the nation. The Prime Minister has categorically stated that until and unless 4 per cent growth in agriculture is achieved the overall growth rate of the economy cannot be sustained. The following table provides an idea on the status of the Indian Agriculture.

**Table 1.1. Production of Cash Crops in India**

| Cash Crops | 1960-61 | 1990-91 | 1999-2000 | 2007-2008 | 2008-2009 |
|---|---|---|---|---|---|
| Oil Seeds (Million Tonnes) | 7 | 19 | 21 | 29 | 28 |

| | | | | | |
|---|---|---|---|---|---|
| Sugar cane (Million Tonnes) | 110 | 254 | 299 | 341 | 285 |
| Cotton (Million bales) | 6 | 10 | 12 | 26 | 22.3 |
| Jute (Million bales) | 4 | 8 | 11 | 11 | 10.4 |
| Potatoes (Million Tonnes) | 3 | 15 | 25 | 28.5 | 29 |

Source: Economic Survey 2009-10

**Table 1.2. Trends in the Production of Food Grains in India**

| Year | Production | Year | Production |
|---|---|---|---|
| 1970-71 | 108 | 2002-03 | 174 |
| 1978-79 | 132 | 2003-04 | 212 |
| 1990-91 | 176 | 2006-07 | 216 |
| 2001-02 | 213 | 2007-08 | 231 |
| | | 2008-09 | 235 |

Source: Economic Survey (Various issues)

The growth rate of production of cash crops between 1960-61 and 1990-91 has been significant. However the growth rate between 1990-91, 2008-09 is marginal and in some crops negative.

Production of food grains has increased in absolute terms but the growth rate of food grains production from 2003-04 onwards is negligible. Production of pulses has been near stagnant.

Indian agriculture is at cross roads as most of the small and marginal farmers have become landless and seek livelihoods by migrating to urban centres. There are suicides, depressions and crop holidays in the agriculturally superior states like Punjab,

Maharastra, Andhra Pradesh and Tamilnadu. Indian agriculture at this point of time suffers from so many weaknesses.

It is still a gamble in the monsoons. New agricultural strategies necessitate heavy investment in seeds, fertilizers, pesticides, water and labour charges have also increased. As the cost of living under the pressure of inflation has been increasing migration of labour to small towns and urban centers in search of work has created problems of labour shortage and small and medium farmers cannot afford the cost of cultivation at present. 6 per cent of the total farmers are big farmers accounting for 40 per cent of all cultivated land in India. Indian agriculture is becoming capitalistic in the hands of the big farmers in many states including Punjab. Retired civil servants, urban based business mans and ex-service man accounting for 3 per cent of total farmers and are in control of 7 per cent of cultivated land in Punjab alone. Indian agriculture has increased interstate and intra state disparities. Institutional reforms are side tracked and owner cultivators are decreasing. Conditions of the small and marginal farmers are deteriorated. The former U.N. Secretary General, U. Thant stated that relative equality in land ownership through land reforms was imperative in developing countries like India. But this caution is being ignored.

Since 2002-03 Indian agriculture has been passing through crisis. Food grains surplus is no more and large import of wheat are being planned. Dependence on imports for basic items like food grains, edible oils is not healthy for a nation like India. Food security strengthens national security. The Prime Minister has repeatedly accepted the Tenth Five Year Plan goal "Agricultural development is central to economic development of the country".

Deceleration in agricultural growth has its impact on employment. Overall employment growth in the economy was 1.74 per cent during 1983 to 1993-94. It slipped to 1.08 per cent during 1993-94 to 2004-05. During this period agricultural employment decreased from 1.41 to 0.63 per cent. This fact indicates steep fall in the growth of employment in agriculture in the post globalisation period. Open unemployment increased sharply during 1993-94 to 2004-05. According to NSS data open unemployment has increased from 7.49 million in 1993-94 to 13.6 million by 2004-05. Ratio of unemployed persons to the labour force (Incidence & unemployment) increased from 1.96 in 1993-94 to 2.39 in 2004-05.

Economic reforms have deepened the crisis in agriculture since 1991. Public investment in agriculture has been declining. Farmers in the dry regions incur debts by investing in ground water resources to seek irrigation facility. Pressure on land in command areas has increased tenancy system. Liberalisation of agricultural trade by 2000 has been encouraging cheap imports. Prices of commercial crops and some plantation crops are fluctuating and the farmers are financially ruined. High yield crops without estimating their suitability to domestic conditions have resulted in instability of output leading to loss of livelihoods. The following table shows the decline in the share of Gross Capital Formation by the Government.

**Table -1.3. Gross Capital Formation (GCF) in Agriculture at Current Prices**

| Year | Total GCF (Rs. Crore) | Public GCF (Rs. Crores) | Private GCF (Rs. Crores) | Share of Public (%) | Share of Private (%) |
|---|---|---|---|---|---|
| 1980-81 | 4342 | 1876 | 2466 | 43.2 | 56.8 |
| 1990-91 | 15839 | 3586 | 12253 | 22.6 | 77.4 |
| 1995-96 | 17392 | 5952 | 11440 | 34.2 | 65.8 |

| | | | | | |
|---|---|---|---|---|---|
| 1999-00 | 50151 | 8670 | 44481 | 17.3 | 82.7 |
| 2000-01 | 46432 | 8176 | 38256 | 17.6 | 82.4 |
| 2001-02 | 60366 | 10353 | 50013 | 17.2 | 82.8 |
| 2002-03 | 61883 | 9564 | 52319 | 15.5 | 84.5 |
| 2003-04 | 61827 | 12218 | 49609 | 19.8 | 80.2 |
| 2004-05 | 70786 | 13610 | 57176 | 19.2 | 80.8 |
| 2005-06 | 83952 | — | — | — | — |

Source: CSO, National Accounts Statistics, Various Years.

Public investment as per the table has been decreasing in its share in the Gross Capital Formation in agriculture. In 2004-05 it was less than half of the 1980-81 share. No doubt, private investment has been increasing. But it is near static between 1990-91 and 2001-02 share then it has started to decline. Farmers with small holdings have no economic viability. They are not in a position to bear the cost of cultivation on commercial lines. They need timely and assured credit at low rates of interest. Rural areas cannot create employment opportunities to provide income to the small and marginal farmer household. Farm and non-farm linkages are very low in the Indian context.

Rural credit is the money that is extended to the farmers, share croppers, tenants, small, marginal and sub marginal cultivators as well as rural and tribal families engaged in a wide variety of farming related occupations. Survey of rural credit in 1950-51 indicates that 93.0 per cent credit needs of the farmers were provided the money lenders. The AIRCSC (All Indian Rural Credit Survey Committee-1954) stated that cooperation has failed but cooperation must succeed. On the recommendation of this committee, the RBI took a series of measures to strengthen cooperative institutions. AIRCSC (1969) recommended the adoption of multi-agency approach to finance rural the rural sector. The Government of India accepted that rural credit could not be met by cooperative societies alone and that the commercial banks should play an important role in the rural sector which resulted in the following initiatives;

- Nationalisation of 14 banks in 1969.
- Setting up of Credit Guarantee Corporation in 1971.
- Setting up of RRB's in 1975
- Second time Nationalisation of 6 banks in 1980.
- Setting up of NABARD in 1982.
- SHGs-Bank Linkage Programme in 1992 by NABARD.
- Introduction of the Concept of Local Area Bank in 1996-97.
- Launching of KCC (Kisan Credit Card) Scheme is1998 by NABARD.
- The concept of Financial Inclusion has been introduced in 11th Five Year Plan.

The Government has initiated some new measures to ensure adequate credit flow in rural areas. 3,25,000 crores was set up as target for agricultural credit flow for the year 2009-10. Debt waiver and debt relief schemes were announced in the budget 2008-09 with an amount Rs.60,000 crores. Marginal farmers and small farmers have been given complete waiver of all loans due on December 31, 2007 and which were not paid until February 29, 2008. For other farmers One Time Settlement Scheme with a rebate of 25 per cent was announced. This is a good scheme to help the farmers who could not repay their loans in time due to floods, drought and unfavourable circumstances. They are able to get fresh credit and cultivate their land. Rehabilitation package with 69,978.69 crores was approved for 31 suicide prone districts in 4 states of Andhra Pradesh, Maharastra, Karnataka and Kerala. The objective of the package was to establish a sustainable and viable farming and livelihood support system through debt relief to farmers, improved supply of institutional credit.

Mechanisms and delivery channels have been created to provide short and long term institutional credit at the reasonable rate of interest to farmers. High rate of interest charged by the non-institutional agencies are to be discouraged by expanding the institutional credit. But credit provided by the cooperatives is negligible and has declined over the period. The share of agriculture credit in total commercial bank credit was above 18 per cent by 1980. It had declined to 11 per cent during 2004 to 2006. The share of RRB's in total agricultural credit at the national level has remained between 6 to 9 per cent during the same period. Among the farmers, marginal and small farmer households have been the worst sufferers. Their share in total number of farmers has been increasing at a fast rate than their share in land.

## Rural Indebtedness

Farmers in India borrow year after year but they are not a position to clear off the loans as their incomes are not sufficient and sometimes uncertain. Non-institutional agencies charge high rates of interest. Interest and principal go on increasing. The debt of the farmers go on increasing year after year and this situation is called Rural Indebtedness.

Rural Indebtedness depends on various factors which influence and reinforce others. Consequently, farmers remain in debt trap. The famous saying "Indian farmer is born in debt lives in debt and dies in debt" is true in letter and spirit.

The extent of rural indebtedness based on NSS $59^{th}$ round is given here under:

**Table 1.4. Amount of debt by occupational categories**

| Year | Amount of Debt (Rs.Crores) | | | Share of Cultivators in (%) | |
|---|---|---|---|---|---|
| | Cultivators | Non-Cultivators | All | Total debt | Total No. of Households |
| 1971 | 3,374 | 474 | 3,848 | 87.7 | 72.4 |
| 1981 | 5,737 | 456 | 6,193 | 92.6 | 76.3 |
| 1991 | 17,668 | 453 | 22,211 | 79.5 | 66.1 |
| 2002 | 81,709 | 29,759 | 1,11,468 | 73.3 | 59.7 |

Source: NSS 59th Round (January-December 2002).

As per the data in the above table total debt of rural household has been increasing over the period 73.3 per cent of total debt pertains to 60 per cent cultivators households. It implies that 40 per cent of non-cultivator households account for just 20 per cent total debt. Incidence of indebtedness is also worked out based on household asset and the percentage share of debt burden among the rural households. Here also NSS data is used:

**Table 1.5. Incidence of Indebtedness of Rural Households in 2002**

| Asset household class (Rs.000) | Incidence of Indebtedness (%) | | |
|---|---|---|---|
| | Institutional | Non-Institutional | Total |
| Less than 15 | 3.6 | 12.0 | 15.0 |
| 15-30 | 6.2 | 13.9 | 19.0 |
| 30-60 | 8.7 | 17.7 | 25.2 |
| 60-100 | 10.9 | 17.7 | 26.5 |
| 100-150 | 13.6 | 17.9 | 28.3 |
| 150-200 | 14.6 | 17.1 | 28.7 |
| 200-300 | 16.2 | 15.7 | 28.7 |
| 300-450 | 18.7 | 13.2 | 28.7 |
| 450-800 | 22.0 | 13.0 | 31.0 |
| 800 and Above | 26.7 | 10.3 | 32.9 |
| All | 13.4 | 15.5 | 26.5 |

Source: NSS 59th Round.

Data in the above table clearly shows that the richer household are more indebted to institutional sources whereas poorer household depends mostly on non-institutional agencies. In other words rich farmers are more benefited from institutional agencies, while the poor farm households owe much to the non-institutional sources at high rates of interest.

NSS data has also revealed that 51.4 per cent of the rural households were not indebted. The average outstanding debt per farmer household was Rs. 12,585 in 2003 against per indebted farmers household was at Rs. 25,902 the share of institutional agencies in the overall debt of the farmers has increased from 17.3 per cent in 1951 to 61.1 per cent in 2002. The share of institutional agencies in 2002 is less than the share in 1981. It implies that the share of non-institutional agencies has been increasing, mostly money lenders between 1991-2002. The following table gives the share of institutional and non-institutional agencies over the period.

**Table 1.6. Share of Debt # of Cultivators Households from Different Sources: 1951-2002**

| Share of Credit | 1951 | 1961 | 1971 | 1981 | 1991 | 2002 |
|---|---|---|---|---|---|---|
| Institutional | 7.3 | 18.7 | 31.7 | 63.2 | 66.3 | 61.1 |
| Cooperative Societies/ Banks etc. | 3.3 | 2.6 | 22.0 | 29.8 | 30.0 | 30.2 |
| Commercial Banks | 0.9 | 0.6 | 2.4 | 28.8 | 35.2 | 26.3 |
| Non-Institutional | 92.7 | 81.3 | 66.3 | 36.8 | 30.6 | 38.9 |
| Money Lenders | 69.7 | 49.2 | 36.1 | 16.1 | 17.5 | 26.8 |
| Unspecified | — | — | — | — | 3.1 | — |
| **Total** | **100.0** | **100.0** | **100.0** | **100.0** | **100.0** | **100.0** |

Source: Reserve Bank of India (RBI), All-India Rural Credit Survey, 1951-52: RBI, All India Rural Debt and Investment Survey, 1961-62 and NSSO, All India Debt and Investment Surveys 1971-72, 1981-82, 1991-92 and 2003.

#Debt refers to outstanding cash dues

It is observed that small and marginal farmer households who accounts for 80 per cent of indebted farmer households account for 51 per cent of the total outstanding credit from institutional agencies. Their dependence on non-institutional agencies is more than that of large farmers. Even cooperatives provide small amount to the marginal farmer driving them to depend on money lenders.

Indebtedness by purpose wise is analysed in the following table:

**Table 1.7. Distribution of Debt by Purpose of Among Rural Cultivator Housholds:1961-2002**

| **Purpose** | **1961** | **1971** | **1981** | **2002** |
|---|---|---|---|---|
| Productive | 40.1 | 54.0 | 71.6 | 62.9 |
| Farm-Business | 36.6 | 49.7 | 63.8 | 52.5 |
| Current Expenditure | 26.8 | 34.7 | 45.3 | 34.3 |
| Non-Farm Business | 9.8 | 15.0 | 18.5 | 18.2 |
| Capital Expenditure | 3.5 | 4.3 | 7.8 | 9.4 |
| Current Expenditure | 1.4 | 3.2 | 6.3 | 7.4 |
| Non-Productive | 2.1 | 1.1 | 1.5 | 2.0 |
| Non-Productive | 60.0 | 46.0 | 28.4 | 38.1 |
| Household Expenditure | 49.2 | 37.8 | 20.0 | 27.7 |
| Other Purposes | 10.8 | 7.2 | 8.4 | 10.4 |
| Repayment of Debt | 5.0 | 1.5 | 0.1 | 1.5 |
| Expenditure on litigation | 1.8 | 0.7 | 0.8 | 0.3 |
| Financial Investment | 0.2 | 0.2 | 1.0 | 0.6 |
| **All Purposes** | **100.0** | **100.0** | **100.0** | **100.0** |

Source: RBI, All India Rural Debt Investment Survey 1961-62 and NSSO, All India Debt and Investment Surveys, 1971-72, 1981-82 and 2003.

It is observed from the above table that the debt for productive purposes in percentage terms has been increasing. It implies that non-productive debt component has decreased over the years. Household expenditure and on other allied items the percentage share is more in the non-productive component.

During the last 10-12 years cost of living has been increasing, conspicuous consumption through media and urban interactions has been increasing. Cost of agricultural inputs has been high. Ambitions and aspirations of the rural people have become high while income from agricultural and non-agricultural sources have been uncertain. Institutions are favourable to the rich.

Small, marginal farmers and agricultural labourers depend on money lenders and are forced to pay high rates of interest. They are getting choked and dazzled by the prevailing situation. Debt – high rate of interest – cumulative amount to principal increase in the outstanding debt move in the form of a vicious circle.

## Reasons for Growing Rural Indebtedness

The main reason of the indebtedness of the farmers is their poverty. Their incomes are low and asset values are low. Past savings of the households are meager. Constant crop failures force them to borrow. Sometimes they taken loan to develop and purchase cattle and agricultural implements. Poverty drives the farmer to borrow and due to poverty they are not able to repay adding interest to the principal.

Agricultural marketing is not remunerative and it every stage there are middle men to sallow a part of farmers income sometimes farmers may borrow to purchase additional land as land ownership is a matter prestige in rural India. They have a strong passion to possess land. Social customs, religious functions, marriages, festivals, child birth, death of family members, guest feeding and the like are all accepted in the traditional rural economy and all these items come under un-productive expenditure. Loans are taken and incomes are not generated to repay.

Sometimes there are court cases even on silly issues in the name of social status and they borrow for legal expenses. It is also un-productive and debt burden increases. The feeling in the rural India is that one should redeem debt of parents. So the inherited debt continuous and adds to the debt flow. Money lenders and micro finance agencies at present are also responsible for rural indebtedness. They charge higher rate of interest add the interest to the principal and ultimately force the borrowers to part with land. Agents of micro finance institutions threaten the farmers and take away some of the assets in the name of repayment. They encourage the farmers first to take loans and then take away the land. Farmers cannot come out the clutches of the money lenders when once loans are taken.

Constant crop failure, cattle death, cattle feed famines are all responsible for growing indebtedness. Technology is fast changing and so are the life styles both in rural and urban India. In the name of modern education, in the name corporate medical treatment, in the line of lavish spending on marriage, rural people barrow mostly and are not in a position to repay. "Some believe in the Karma Doctrine" and allow things to drift away. Rural atmosphere is also vitiated with different vices like gambling, alcohol addiction for which barrowing is the only means. Six reasons are attributed for the death of the great Mahabharath warrior, Karna and similarly rural indebtedness is the result of many factors.

## Implications of Rural Indebtedness

Increasing rural indebtedness pauperisus the small and marginal farmers year after year. Interest payments accumulate and their incomes are eroded. Normally small and marginal farmers mortgage their land to the money lenders or other non-institutional agencies and ultimately they lose their land and become land less labourers. Weaker sections of the farming community get lower prices while selling their produce to the commission agents, traders and middleman to clear of a part of the debt. Therefore, rural indebtedness is the cause and effect of the growing poverty of the Indian farmers. Indebtedness creates psychological problems like depression, loss of interest in agriculture and frustration resulting in low concentration on agriculture. Agricultural production is thus effected. The bargaining power of the indebted rural household becomes weak and economic transactions are always not beneficial to them.

Rural indebtedness adds to the class of landless labourers and tenants by changing the social status of independent farmers. There are some examples in Punjab where the landless labourers pledge themselves for loans and become bonded labourers to the landlords and money lenders. Rural indebtedness creates social unrest as the money lenders and non-institutional agencies usurp the land of the small farmers fraudulently. Illiteracy, ignorance and denial of institutional loans force them to go to the money lenders or big land lords. Such problems have been reported in states like Bihar, Orissa, Punjab, Haryana and in parts of Andhra Pradesh. Rural indebtedness creates social inferiority and economic insecurity. The small barrowers cannot face the threats and eviction measures of the money lenders. In the social outlook indebted farm household face a degraded image. Domestic peace is distributed and future planning cannot be made.

Rural indebtedness is one of the reasons for the growing suicides of farmers. Empirical evidence reveals such deaths in the agriculturally advanced states like Punjab, Haryana, Maharashtra, Tamil Nadu, Kerala and Andhra Pradesh. Overall health of the indebted farmers is effected and the charm of life loses its shine. They may suffer from frequent depressions and are easily irritable.

Rural indebtedness encourages migration to urban centers to seek the livelihood. The migrated usually do not have proper skills suited for the urban needs. They remain casual labourers in the buzz of the urban life without basic needs of life. As cost of cultivation is increasing and agricultural incomes are uncertain some small and marginal farmers declare "Crop Holiday". It implies land, the most valuable natural resource, remains unutilised and it is a national waste of resource.

Rural indebtedness tells upon the overall personality of the borrowers. It's cancerous effects spread over the family members of the indebted household. The customary social norm in rural India is "No borrowing for the Dal Rice". It implies traditions ordain the Indians to live within means and not to go in search of lush, green fields in dream like situations.

## Significance of the Study

This study "Rural Indebtedness of Weaker Sections in Telangana" analyses the chronic melody that has been effecting the very vitals of the rural community, especially, the farming community. The weaker sections SC, ST and BC farmers suffer more as their land holdings are marginal and small. Non-farm employment opportunities and income generation activities are meager in the rural setup. Expansion of institutional agencies of credit has been spectacular both in volume and diffusion. But these sections hover around the non-institutional sources, particularly, money lenders for their credit needs unmindful of the consequences weaker sections of the rural areas comprising marginal and small farmers, artisans and land less labourers groan under the growing burden of the debt. These sections are highly inaccessible to the institutional credit in view of their poverty, near zero level asset base, ignorance and illiteracy. But these vulnerable sections have to invest more on production, marketing and consumption in the light of the rising inflation amidst the changes in and around the economy under the thrust of globalisation and the resultant techno changes. Consumption patterns, basket of goods, investment costs and inputs, nature and cost of child education, health expenditure and of every item of personal, social and economic life of the rural societies has under gone radical change and overall expenditure have shown upward movements. Incomes from agricultural produce are uncertain as the produce and the market prices are always uncertain. These sections are driven by compulsion to depend on the money lenders and private financial agencies, MFIs and middle men. They bear the brunt of the debt burden and remain helpless in the debt trap, live in the debt trap and leave the families in the slush of debt. Implications of indebtedness and stories of misery are untold in different parts of the country. Suicide attempts, suicides, social unrest, health problems, crop holidays are all on the increase and demanding the attention of the policy makers, academicians, civil society organisations.

In this context the present study attempts to explore the daunting problems of rural indebtedness from close corners in its depth by taking two adjoining districts i.e., Khammam and Warangal of the Telangana Region of Andhra Pradesh. Both the districts are included in the 31 districts identified for the Prime Ministers package of Rs. 100 crores. The study concentrates only on the weaker sections and analyses the inter-district and intra-district facets of the problem of the indebtedness.

### Scope of the Study

Khamman and Warangal districts of Telangana Region have been taken for the study. 6 mandals, 3 from each district and 2 villages from each mandal comprising 300 respondents are analysed. After analysing the socio-economic conditions in the study area sources of the credit and credit flow are estimated. Caste category wise perception applied to identify the weaker sections for the analysis. Indebtedness is estimated in relation to land ownership, caste, asset and income levels and per household indebted quantum also been worked out. Utilisation of the credit purpose wise is examined. Implications of indebtedness from social, economic and personal points of view are examined.

### Methodology-Objectives

1. To examine the socio-economic conditions of the weaker sections in the study area.
2. To assess the share of institutional and non-institutional sources in the flow of credit to the respondent households.
3. To quantify the overall debt burden of the respondent households.
4. To analyse the utilisation of debt by the respondents.

5. To estimate the implications of indebtedness from different points of view.
6. To propose valid suggestions to the policy makers.

## Hypotheses

1. Incidence of rural indebtedness is more among the weaker sections with variations from caste to caste.
2. Institutional credit is positively correlated with the socio-economic status of the rural households. In other words medium and big farmers have more access to the institutional credit than the small and marginal farmers.
3. Rural indebtedness in its implications, pervade the overall living conditions of the borrowers, sometimes, posing a threat to the very existence.

Connectivities from the above hypotheses are:

a. Among the weaker sections BCs may be in a better situation than SC and ST respondents.
b. Incidence of indebtedness to a large extent is high among the weaker sections of the farming community.
c. Rich farmers with large land holding are capable of getting more credit from banks and other institutions. Small and marginal farmers are in the neglected lot.
d. Rural indebtedness has far reaching consequences including threats to life. It engulfs social, political, economic and domestic spheres of the borrowers.

## Sample Design

The two districts, Warangal and Khammam, identified among the 37 districts for the Prime Minister's Relief Package are taken as sample districts purposefully. Mandal wise population of BC,

SC and ST are observed in each district. The mandals with maximum percentage of BC, SC and ST population are selected purposefully as the study focuses on weaker sections. So in each district the selected mandals have particular backward caste to the maximum in percentage terms. Within a mandal two villages are selected randomly and 25 respondents from each village are selected by following random sampling method. As such the respondents from a village represent all the castes with a particular caste to the maximum. The 300 respondents in their study comprise BC, SC and ST and are close in number.

The following table shows the overall sample district wise, mandal wise, village wise and castes.

**Table-1.8. Particulars of the Sample Respondents**

| Name of the District | Name of the Mandal | Name of the Village | Castes | | | Total |
|---|---|---|---|---|---|---|
| | | | BC | SC | ST | |
| Warangal | Geesugonda | Sthambampally | 16 | 09 | 0 | 25 |
| | | Kommla | 18 | 07 | 0 | 25 |
| | Hasaparthy | Devannapeta | 10 | 15 | 0 | 25 |
| | | Chinthagattu | 06 | 19 | 0 | 25 |
| | Kuravi | Rajole | 03 | 04 | 18 | 25 |
| | | Gundrathimadugu | 02 | 03 | 20 | 25 |
| Khammam | Karepally | Usirikayalapally | 16 | 04 | 05 | 25 |
| | | Seetharampur | 18 | 04 | 03 | 25 |
| | Tekulapalle | Bodu | 03 | 06 | 16 | 25 |
| | | Koppurai | 01 | 06 | 18 | 25 |
| | Bonakal | Thutikunta | 05 | 15 | 05 | 25 |
| | | Laxmipuram | 03 | 20 | 02 | 25 |
| **Total** | | | **101** | **112** | **87** | **300** |

Source: Field Study

## Data Collection

Both primary and secondary data are collected for this study. Primary data has been collected by administering a structured questionnaire (Schedule) and the responses were recorded. While collecting information the researcher has noted down separately other details given by the respondents relevant to the study. Secondary data sources include books, journals and reports of the special committees and commissions. Season and crop reports published by the Bureau of Economics and Statistics, Government of Andhra Pradesh and India. Publications of the National Institute of Rural Development, Indian Journal of Agricultural Economics, Survey Reports and the recent Radha Krishnan Committee Report on Rural Indebtedness have been studied to strengthen the analysis. District level Annual Statistics published by the collectorates and the District Planning wings are also used as secondary sources.

## Statistical Tools Used

Data collected from field investigation has been coded and processed in simple frequency and Cross Tabulation, Simple Averages and Percentages are worked out for intra and inter data comparisons of the analysis. Quotients, indicators and ratios are also used to sum up/ simplify the analysis. Diagrams to show the relative weightage are also used as per the necessity. Scaling technique in simple format is used.

## Limitations

1. This research study is carried out in two adjoining districts of the Telangana Region. The observations may/may not be generalised in view of the limited coverage.

2. This study taken only the weaker sections viz., BC, SC and ST respondents. As such the conclusion may not give a complete picture of the overall debt scenario.
3. Most of the respondents, in this study, are farmers and so other sections of the rural society remain outside the ambit. Hence the conclusions may not be generalised for the total rural set up.
4. Data collected pertains to a point of time but not over a period time making it unable to examine the trends.
5. Most of the respondents are illiterate and as such the responses depend on their ability to recall. The general practice among the Indian households, more so, in the rural areas is not to maintain accounts.
6. Responses may not be accurate in view of the shunned nature of the rural society with regard to financial issues, like outstanding indebted quantum's.

Even then, this research study seeks to find out certain issues, identify the basic problems and highlight the important areas of concern which will be of immense use to the policy makers, researchers and agencies concerned with Agricultural Development and Rural Welfare.

## Chapterisation

This study is divided into six chapters. Chapter one, the present one is Introduction and Methodology where in the problem of Rural Indebtedness is analysed and the Research Process, in its constructs is explained. Second chapter deals with the earlier studies on the problem to enable the researcher acquainted with contents, techniques and gaps. This chapter also helps to fit in the findings of this research work into the body of knowledge already accumulated. Profiles of the sample districts, mandals and villages examine the base level conditions of the study area. Socio-economic conditions of the respondents are analysed in the third chapter from which the spurt in the economic activities can be estimated. Rural Indebtedness is established and it is quantified in the fourth chapter along with the Institutional credit flow to the respondents. Utilisation of credit for different purposes by the respondents is examined in the fifth chapter along with the Implications of Rural Indebtedness from different dimensions credit, by itself, is not harmful. If used properly income is generated by creating surplus from which debts and interest accrued can be cleared off and this aspect is also explored. Summary conclusions and suggestions emerging out of this research study based on empirical verification are given in the sixth/final chapter.

# 2

# Socio-Economic Conditions of the Study Area

Economic activities are the interactions between the human resource and the natural resources within the given techno sphere with the available capital stock. In all such interactions socio-economic cultural and psychological factors play a determining role in all stages of the economic pursuits. Socio-economic conditions of the study area are analysed in this chapter, district wise, as the study extends to two adjoining districts. This approach of separate analysis helps to identify the differences or similarities between the areas of proximity, too. 150 respondents are selected from six villages, two each, from three mandals in each district.

## A. Warangal District

**Table-2.1. Caste-wise particulars of the respondents**

| Name of the Village | Name of the Mandal | BC | SC | ST | Total |
|---|---|---|---|---|---|
| Sthambampally | Geesugonda | 16 (29.0) | 09 (15.7) | (0.00) | 25 (16.66) |
| Komala | | 18 (32.7) | 07 (12.2) | (0.00) | 25 (16.66) |
| Devannapeta | Hasanparthy | 10 (18.1) | 15 (26.3) | (0.00) | 25 (16.66) |
| Chinthagattu | | 06 (10.9) | 19 (33.3) | (0.00) | 25 (16.66) |

| | | | | | |
|---|---|---|---|---|---|
| Rajolu | Kuravi | 03 (5.4) | 04 (7.0) | 18 (47.3) | 25 (16.66) |
| Gundrathimadugu | | 02 (3.6) | 03 (5.2) | 20 (52.6) | 25 (16.66) |
| **Total** | | **55 (36.67)** | **57 (38.00)** | **38 (25.33)** | **150 (100.0)** |

Source: Field Study

As per the above table 55(36.67) respondents are BCs, 57(38.0) are SCs and the remaining 38(25.33) respondents are STs. It is observable in the table that BCs are more 62 percent in one mandal, Geesugonda while SCs are more 59 percent in Hasanparthy Mandal. STs are totally present in Kuravi Mandal only implying that they are not spread to other mandals BCs and SCs co-exist in all mandals in degrees whereas STs are confined to the two villages of a single mandal. Data in the above table represents the weaker sections of the agrarian economy, each section being dominant in a mandal.

**Table-2.2. Caste-wise age particulars of the respondents**

| **Caste** | **20-30** | **30-40** | **40-50** | **50-60** | **Above 60** | **Total** |
|---|---|---|---|---|---|---|
| BC | 05 (50.0) | 10 (37.0) | 22 (34.3) | 16 (38.0) | 02 (28.5) | 55 (36.67) |
| SC | 04 (40.0) | 12 (44.4) | 20 (31.2) | 19 (45.2) | 02 (28.5) | 57 (38.00) |
| ST | 01 (10.0) | 05 (18.5) | 22 (34.3) | 07 (16.6) | 03 (42.8) | 38 (25.33) |
| **Total** | **10 (6.7)** | **27 (18.0)** | **64 (42.6)** | **42 (28.0)** | **07 (4.6)** | **150 (100.000** |

Source: Field Study

Age particulars of the respondents, caste wise, are given in the above table. 133(88.6) respondents are in the 30-60 years age group. It is a welcome feature since this group has all the vitality to carry on agriculture. 10(6.7) respondents are below 30 years while 7(4.6) respondents are above 60 years. It is interesting to note from the table that more than 50% of the ST respondents are in the 40-50 years group unlike the other two groups. Of course, the dominant age group among all castes is 40-50. Age in terms of experience, physical stamina has a telling effect on the efficiency of the individual.

**Table-2.3. Caste-wise literacy particulars of the respondents**

| Caste | Literates | Illiterates | Total |
|---|---|---|---|
| BC | 32 (51.1) | 23 (26.1) | 55 (36.67) |
| SC | 16 (25.8) | 41 (46.5) | 57 (38.00) |
| ST | 14 (22.5) | 24 (27.2) | 38 (25.33) |
| **Total** | **62 (21.3)** | **88 (58.6)** | **150 (100.00)** |

Source: Field Study

32 (51.0) BC respondents are literates followed by 16 (25.8) SC respondents and only 14 (22.5) of the ST respondents. Only 62 (41.3) of the respondents are literates while 88 (58.6) are illiterates. Around 64 percent of the ST respondents are illiterates. If illiteracy is taken as one of the indicators of backwardness. SCs come first followed by STs and BCs. Even among BC respondent's illiteracy is 42%. Illiteracy has become a stumbling block in bringing the rural economy on to the road of development.

**Table-2.4. Caste-wise education levels of the respondents**

| Caste | Primary | Secondary | Higher secondary | Total |
|---|---|---|---|---|
| BC | 23 (53.4) | 05 (45.4) | 04 (50.0) | 32 (51.6) |
| SC | 09 (20.9) | 04 (36.3) | 03 (37.5) | 16(25.8) |
| ST | 11 (25.5) | 02 (18.1) | 01 (12.5) | 14 (22.5) |
| **Total** | **43 (69.3)** | **11 (17.7)** | **08 (12.9)** | **62 (100.0)** |

Source: Field Study

More than half of the literate respondents are BCs while the SCs and ST respondents share the remaining half. Levels of education, caste wise, indicate that BCs come first followed by SC and ST respondents.

**Table-2.5. School going children of the respondent households**

| Name of the Village | Name of the Mandal | School going children | | | Total |
|---|---|---|---|---|---|
| | | BC | SC | ST | |
| Sthambampally | Geesukonda | 15 (18.7) | 12 (19.7) | 8 (18.1) | 35 (18.9) |
| Kommala | | 11 (13.7) | 9 (14.7) | 9 (20.4) | 29 (15.7) |
| Devannapeta | Hasanparthy | 16 (20.0) | 14 (22.9) | 7 (15.9) | 37 (20.0) |
| Chintagattu | | 18 (22.5) | 15 (24.5) | 10 (22.7) | 43 (23.2) |
| Rajolu | Kuravi | 12 (15.0) | 6 (9.8) | 7 (15.9) | 25 (13.5) |
| Gundratimadugu | | 8 (10.0) | 5 (8.1) | 3 (6.8) | 16 (8.6) |
| **Total** | | **80 (43.2)** | **61 (32.9)** | **44 (23.7)** | **185 (100.0)** |

Source: Field study

School going children of the respondents households are 185. Children of BC respondents are 80, SC respondents 61 and ST respondents are 44. Children among the total population of 670 are 27.6 per cent.

**Table-2.6. School Drop-outs of the respondent households**

| Name of the Village | Name of the Mandal | School Drop-outs | | | Total |
|---|---|---|---|---|---|
| | | BC | SC | ST | |
| Sthambampally | Geesukonda | 1 (20.0) | 1 (16.6) | 1 (12.5) | 3 (15.7) |
| Kommala | | 1 (20.0) | — | 1 (12.5) | 2 (10.5) |
| Devannapeta | Hasanparthy | 1 (20.0) | 1 (16.6) | — | 2 (10.5) |
| Chintagattu | | — | 1 (16.6) | 1 (12.5) | 2 (10.5) |
| Rajolu | Kuravi | 1 (20.0) | 1 (16.6) | 2 (25.0) | 4 (21.0) |

| Gundratimadugu | | 1 (20.0) | 2 (33.3) | 3 (37.5) | 6 (31.5) |
|---|---|---|---|---|---|
| **Total** | | **5 (26.3)** | **6 (31.5)** | **8 (42.1)** | **19 (100.0)** |

Source: Field study

166 children go to school and there are 19 school drop-outs. In per cent terms 10.2 per cent of the school age children are not in schools. There are drop-outs in all castes. However, school drop-outs are more among ST children.

**Table-2.7. Sex-wise distribution of the respondent households**

| Name of the Village | Name of the Mandal | Sex-wise distribution | | | | | | Total |
|---|---|---|---|---|---|---|---|---|
| | | BC | | SC | | ST | | |
| | | M | F | M | F | M | F | |
| Sthamba-m-pally | Geesu-konda | 15 (30.7) | 1 (16.7) | 7 (14.8) | 2 (20.0) | ___ | ___ | 25 (16.6) |
| Kommala | | 16 (32.7) | 2 (33.3) | 6 (12.7) | 1 (10.0) | ___ | ___ | 25 (16.6) |
| Devannapeta | Hasan-parthy | 10 (20.4) | ___ | 13 (27.6) | 2 (20.0) | ___ | ___ | 25 (16.6) |
| Chin-tagattu | | 4 (8.1) | 2 (33.3) | 16 (34.0) | 3 (30.0) | ___ | ___ | 25 (16.6) |
| Rajolu | Kuravi | 3 (6.1) | ___ | 3 (6.3) | 1 (10.0) | 13 (50.0) | 5 (41.7) | 25 (16.6) |
| Gundrati-madugu | | 1 (20.4) | 1 (16.7) | 2 (4.2) | 1 (10.0) | 13 (50.0) | 7 (58.3) | 25 (16.6) |
| **Total** | | **49 (32.7)** | **6 (4.0)** | **47 (31.3)** | **10 (6.7)** | **26 (17.3)** | **12 (8.0)** | **150 (100.0)** |

Source: Field study

122 respondents are males and remaining 22 are females. Female respondents are more 12 among STs followed by SCs 10 and BCs 6 in percentage terms male respondents are 81.4 and female respondents are 18.6 per cent as given in the above table.

**Table- 2.8. Caste-wise type of the family of the respondents**

| Caste | Joint | Nuclear | Total |
|---|---|---|---|
| BC | 28 (48.2) | 27 (29.3) | 55 (36.67) |
| SC | 21 (36.2) | 36 (39.1) | 57 (38.00) |
| ST | 09 (15.5) | 29 (31.5) | 38 (25.33) |
| **Total** | **58 (38.6)** | **92 (61.3)** | **150 (100.0)** |

Source: Field Study

Caste wise breakup of the families of the respondents indicate that 28 (51.0) BC respondents prefer joint families. 37 percent SC respondents and 24 percent ST respondents opt for joint families. It implies that Nuclear families are more preferred by ST families.

**Table-2.9. Caste-wise occupational particulars of the respondents**

| Caste | Agriculture | Non-agriculture | Total |
|---|---|---|---|
| BC | 55 (36.6) | (0.00) | 55 (36.6) |
| SC | 57 (38.0) | (0.00) | 57 (38.0) |
| ST | 38 (25.3) | (0.00) | 38 (25.3) |
| **Total** | **150 (100.0)** | **(0.00)** | **150 (100.0)** |

Source: Field Study

All the respondents from all the villages in the district of study have agriculture as the main occupation. Selection of the sample respondents is purposeful in this aspect and as such primary occupation village wise and caste wise of the respondents is agriculture. The study seeks to focus on the weaker sections and so SC, ST and BC respondents alone are taken.

**Table-2.10. Caste-wise category particulars of the respondents**

| Caste | M.F | S.F | Mid. F | B.F | Total |
|---|---|---|---|---|---|
| BC | 29 (46.0) | 16 (26.6) | 07 (36.8) | 03 (37.5) | 55 (36.6) |
| SC | 24 (38.0) | 26 (43.3) | 05 (26.3) | 02 (25.0) | 57 (38.0) |
| ST | 10 (15.8) | 18 (30.0) | 07 (36.8) | 03 (37.5) | 38 (25.3) |
| **Total** | **63 (42.0)** | **60 (40.0)** | **19 (12.6)** | **08 (5.3)** | **150 (100.0)** |

Source: Field Study

Marginal farmers are more, 29 (53.0) among BCs followed by SCs 42 percent and STs 27 percent. In other words STs are better than the other two categories in holding land. Around 47 percent of the ST respondents are small farmers while 45.6 percent the BCs are in this category. Around 30 percent of the BCs are small farmers. It implies that more BC respondents are marginal farmers. BC and ST respondents are more than SCs with regard to medium and big farmers.

**Table-2.11. Land particulars of the respondents**

| Caste | Own | Leased | Both | Total |
|---|---|---|---|---|
| BC | 38 (37.6) | 10 (38.4) | 07 (30.4) | 55 (36.6) |
| SC | 36 (35.6) | 09 (34.6) | 12 (52.1) | 57 (38.0) |
| ST | 27 (26.7) | 07 (26.9) | 04 (17.3) | 38 (25.3) |
| **Total** | **101 (56.2)** | **26 (17.33)** | **23 (15.33)** | **150 (100.0)** |

Source: Field study

26 (17.33) of the respondents depend exclusively on leased land. More than half 101 (56.2) of the respondents have own land while 23 (15.33) have both own and leased lands. Interestingly 83 percent of the respondents have own land. In other words absentee landlordism still exists to a considerable extent as shown in the table.

**Table-2.12. Particulars of the land by the respondents (in acres)**

| Caste | Wet land | Dry land | Total land |
|---|---|---|---|
| BC | 121 (35.9) | 92 (35.1) | 213 (35.5) |
| SC | 113 (33.5) | 75 (28.6) | 188 (31.3) |
| ST | 103 (30.5) | 95 (36.2) | 198 (33.0) |
| **Total** | **337 (56.2)** | **262 (43.7)** | **599 (100.0)** |

Source: Field study

Total area of land in the study read599 acres ofwhich 337 acres (56.2) are wet and the remaining 262 acres (43.7) are dry. BCs possess more wet land 121(35.9) followed by SCs 113 (33.5) acres and STs 103 (30.5) acres. STs have more dry land 95 (36.2) acres followed by BCs 92 (35.1) acres and SCs 75 (28.6) acres.

**Table-2.13. Particulars of irrigation facilities**

| Caste | Yes | No | Total |
|---|---|---|---|
| BC | 30 (36.1) | 25 (37.3) | 55 (36.6) |
| SC | 34 (40.9) | 23 (34.3) | 57 (38.0) |
| ST | 19 (22.8) | 19 (28.3) | 38 (25.3) |
| **Total** | **83 (55.3)** | **67 (44.6)** | **150 (100.0)** |

Source: Field study

83 (55.3) respondents have irrigation facilities. 34 SC respondents (60.0), 30 (54.5) BC respondents and 19 (50.0) ST respondents have irrigation facilities. It implies that more than half of the respondents is each category enjoy irrigation facilities as given here under.

**Table-2.14. Particulars of source-wise irrigation**

| Caste | Canal | Tanks | Open wells | Bore wells | More than one | Total |
|---|---|---|---|---|---|---|
| BC | 14 (36.8) | 02 (18.1) | 08 (38.0) | 01 (50.0) | 05 (45.4) | 30 (36.1) |
| SC | 16 (42.1) | 04 (36.3) | 09 (42.8) | 01 (50.0) | 04 (36.3) | 34 (40.9) |
| ST | 08 (21.0) | 05 (45.4) | 04 (19.0) | (0.00) | 02 (18.1) | 19 (22.8) |
| **Total** | **38 (45.7)** | **11 (13.2)** | **21 (25.3)** | **02 (2.4)** | **11 (13.2)** | **83 (100.0)** |

Source: Field study

Data in the above table clearly states that bore well irrigation is insignificant. Canals come first covering 38 (45.7) respondents followed by open wells 21(25.3) and tanks 11 (13.2) respondents depend on more than one source to irrigation land. Canals are important source to all castes. No ST respondent has borne well.

**Table-2.15. Means of the irrigation by the respondent**

| Caste | Electrical Motors | Direct canal | Total |
|---|---|---|---|
| BC | 11 (30.5) | 19 (40.4) | 30 (36.1) |
| SC | 16 (44.4) | 18 (38.2) | 34 (40.9) |
| ST | 09 (25.0) | 10 (21.2) | 19 (22.8) |
| **Total** | **36 (43.3)** | **45 (56.7)** | **83 (100.0)** |

Source: Field study

Electrical motors are used for irrigation by 36 (43.3) respondents 16 (44.4%) SC respondents possess electrical motors. Direct canal water is available to 19 (40.4%) BC respondents. Since ST respondents have low irrigation facilities electrical motors are confined to 9 respondents only.

**Table-2.16. Crop-wise particulars of the respondents**

| Caste | BC | SC | ST | Total |
|---|---|---|---|---|
| Paddy | 10 (18.1) | 13 (22.8) | 08 (21.5) | 31 (20.6) |
| Cotton | 12 (21.8) | 09 (15.7) | 05 (13.1) | 26 (17.3) |
| Both | 23 (41.8) | 19 (33.3) | 07 (18.4) | 49 (32.6) |
| Turmeric | 02 (3.6) | 03 (5.2) | - (0.00) | 05 (3.3) |
| Chilly | 05 (9.0) | 02 (3.5) | 13 (34.2) | 20 (13.3) |
| Mize | 02 (3.6) | 04 (7.0) | 04 (10.5) | 10 (6.6) |
| Red gram | 01 (1.8) | - (0.00) | 01 (2.6) | 02 (1.3) |
| Vegetables | - (0.00) | 07 (12.2) | -(0.00) | 07 (4.6) |
| **Total** | **55 (36.6)** | **57 (38.0)** | **38 (25.3)** | **150 (100.0)** |

Source: Field study

Paddy is cultivated by 31 (20.6%) respondents while cotton by 26 (17.3%) respondents. Both paddy and cotton are cultivated by 49 (32.6%) respondents. It implies that 106 respondents out of 150 are in the cultivation of paddy and cotton. They are important crops. Then comes chilly as a commercial crop. Warangal district is known for producing quality chilies. 20 (13.3%) respondents are in the chilly cultivation. ST respondents, 13, are dominant in the chilly cultivation. Maize, vegetables, turmeric and red gram are also cultivated by some respondents. Crop pattern in the study area covers both food and non-food crops. SC respondents alone take up vegetable cultivation. SC respondents are far from turmeric cultivation.

**Table-2.17. Particulars of crop-wise farm size of the respondents**

| Caste | Crops | Paddy | Cotton | Turmeric | Chilly | Mize | Red gram | Vegetables | Total |
|---|---|---|---|---|---|---|---|---|---|
| BC | Respondents | 18 (32.7) | 27 (49.0) | 02 (3.6) | 05 (9.0) | 02 (3.6) | 01 (1.8) | - (0.00) | 55 (100.0) |
| | Area | 62 (29.1) | 130 (61.0) | 04 (1.8) | 11 (5.1) | 05 (2.3) | 01 (0.4) | - (0.00) | 213 (100.0) |
| | Farm size | 3.4 | 4.8 | 2.0 | 2.2 | 2.5 | 1.0 | - | 3.8 |
| SC | Respondents | 22 (38.5) | 19 (33.3) | 03 (5.2) | 02 (3.5) | 04 (7.0) | -(0.00) | 07 (12.2) | 57 (100.0) |
| | Area | 90 (47.8) | 65 (34.5) | 05 (2.6) | 06 (3.1) | 14 (7.4) | - (0.00) | 08 (4.2) | 188 (100.0) |
| | Farm size | 4.0 | 3.4 | 1.6 | 3.0 | 3.5 | - | 1.1 | 3.2 |
| ST | Respondents | 12 (31.5) | 08 (21.0) | (0.00) | 13 (34.2) | 04 (10.5) | 01 (2.6) | -(0.00) | 38 (100.0) |
| | Area | 76 (38.3) | 80 (40.0) | (0.00) | 24 (12.1) | 16 (8.0) | 02 (1.0) | (0.00) | 198 (100.0) |
| | Farm size | 6.3 | 10.0 | - | 1.8 | 4.0 | 2.0 | - | 5.2 |
| **Total** | **Respondents** | **52 (34.6)** | **54 (36.0)** | **05 (3.3)** | **20 (13.3)** | **10 (6.6)** | **02 (1.3)** | **07 (4.6)** | **150 (100.0)** |
| | **Area** | **228 (38.0)** | **275 (45.9)** | **09 (1.5)** | **41 (6.8)** | **35 (5.8)** | **03 (0.5)** | **08 (1.3)** | **599 (100.0)** |
| | **Farm size** | **4.3** | **5.0** | **1.8** | **2.0** | **3.5** | **1.5** | **1.1** | **3.9** |

Source: Field study

Crop wise, farm size of the respondents caste wise, is worked out. It is observed that the farm sizes under paddy crop are 3.4 acres, 4 acres and 6.3 acres for BC, SC, ST respondents respectively. Average farm size under paddy is 4.3 acres in the study area. Average farm size for cotton cultivation in the study area is 5 acres. Farm size of the BC respondents in cotton crop is 4.8 acres which is less than the average and that of the SCs is 3.4 acres also less than the average. However, ST respondents on an average, have 10 acres under cotton crop. BC and SC respondents have more than the average farm size of the study area under chilies. ST respondents allocate more than the average size under maize crop. Average farm size, except under cotton is less than 5 acres under all other crops. However, ST respondents possess larger farms both in paddy and cotton in view of large area under their disposal.

**Table-2.18. Particulars of farm size under food and commercial crops**

| | Food crops | | | Commercial crops | | |
|---|---|---|---|---|---|---|
| **Caste** | **Resp-ondents** | **Area** | **Farm size** | **Respo-ndents** | **Area** | **Farm size** |
| BC | 24 (37.5) | 110 (40.1) | 5.00 | 31 (36.0) | 103 (31.6) | 3.32 |
| SC | 23 (35.9) | 84 (30.6) | 3.65 | 34 (39.5) | 104 (32.0) | 3.05 |
| ST | 17 (26.5) | 80 (29.1) | 4.70 | 21 (24.4) | 118 (36.3) | 5.61 |
| **Total** | **64 (100.0)** | **274 (100.0)** | **4.28** | **86 (100.0)** | **325 (100.0)** | **3.77** |
| | | 150 | | | 150 | |

Source: Field study

Particulars of farm size under food and non-food crops are worked out in the above table. It is a customary practice to allocate more land for food crops by small and marginal farmers in view of personal consumption. The same practice is followed here. The average farm size under food crops is 4.28 acres for the study area as whole. The average farm size of the non-food crops is 3.77 acres. However, there are variations from caste to caste. BC respondents have more irrigation facilities and as such the average farm size of BC respondents under food crops is 5 acres. ST respondents possess more land than the other two castes. Hence, the farm size under non-food crops of the ST respondents is 5.6 acres, higher than the overall average of 3.77 acres.

**Table-2.19. Average expenditure on food crops per acre**

| Caste | BC | SC | ST | Total |
|---|---|---|---|---|
| Area in acres | 110 (40.1) | 84 (30.6) | 80 (29.1) | 274 (100.0) |
| Expenditure on cultivation | 456500 (45.6) | 310800 (31.1) | 232000 (23.2) | 999300 (100.0) |
| Average expenditure | 4150 | 3700 | 2900 | 3647.0 |
| Expenditure on seeds | 77000 (40.1) | 58800 (30.6) | 56000 (29.1) | 191800 (100.0) |
| Average expenditure | 700 | 700 | 700 | 700.0 |
| Expenditure on fertilizer | 308000 (42.4) | 218400 (30.0) | 199200 (27.4) | 725600 (100.0) |
| Average expenditure | 2800 | 2600 | 2490 | 2648.1 |
| Expenditure on pesticides | 1045500 (42.6) | 74760 (30.5) | 65600 (26.7) | 244860 (100.0) |
| Average expenditure | 950 | 890 | 820 | 893.6 |
| Expenditure on irrigation | 132000 (50.1) | 79800 (30.3) | 51200 (19.4) | 263000 (100.0) |
| Average expenditure | 1200 | 950 | 640 | 959.8 |
| Expenditure on labour charges | 588500 (46.0) | 397320 (31.0) | 292000 (22.8) | 1277820 (100.0) |
| Average expenditure | 5350 | 4730 | 3650 | 4663.5 |
| **Total expenditure** | **1666500 (45.0)** | **1139880 (30.7)** | **896000 (24.2)** | **3702380 (100.0)** |
| **Average expenditure** | **15150** | **13570** | **11200** | **13512.3** |

Source: Field study

Cost of cultivation in the farm of expenditure per acre for food crops is examined in the above table. Per acre expenditure on food crops in the study area, on an average is Rs. 13,512.3. It is higher Rs. 15,150 with regard to BC respondents and Rs. 13,570 for SC respondents. Expenditure is less than the average for ST respondents at Rs. 11, 200. Computation of expenditure depends on the prevailing prices at that point of time when computation takes place.

Item wise labour charges come first for all castes. They are a little bit low for ST respondents as the low wage rate in the tribal areas and family labour component influence them. The next item in importance is the cost of cultivation. Cost of cultivation implies preparation of the land through ploughing and other operations. Expenditure on fertilizers is also considerable; wages for family labour are worked out and included in the labour charges.

**T.able-2.20. Yield and Income particulars of the food crops**

| Caste | Area in acres | Total yield | Average yield | Average price | Total income | Average income |
|---|---|---|---|---|---|---|
| BC | 110 (40.1) | 2099 (42.7) | 19.0 | 1000 | 2099000 (43.3) | 19081 |
| SC | 84 (30.6) | 1510 (30.7) | 17.9 | 990 | 1494900 (30.8) | 17796 |
| ST | 80 (29.1) | 1300 (26.4) | 16.2 | 970 | 1261000 (26.0) | 15762 |
| **Total** | **274 (100.0)** | **4909 (100.0)** | **17.9** | **986** | **4840274 (100.0)** | **17665** |

Source : Field study

Yield and income from food crops are examined in the above table. Average yield per acre is 17.9 quintals. Average income from food crops per acre is Rs. 17,665. Yield is multiplied by the average price to arrive at yield in monetary value. BC respondents generate Rs. 19,081 per acre from food crops which is higher than the overall average value. SC respondents also have more than the average yield at Rs. 17,796 per acre. ST respondents are in a disadvantageous position with less than the average yield value at Rs. 15,762.

**Table-2.21. Average expenditure on commercial crops per acre**

| Caste | BC | SC | ST | Total |
|---|---|---|---|---|
| Area in acres | 103 (31.6) | 104 (32.0) | 118 (36.3) | 325 (100.0) |
| Expenditure on cultivation | 525300 (32.0) | 530400 (32.3) | 584100 (35.6) | 1639800 (100.0) |
| Average expenditure | 5100 | 5100 | 4950 | 5045.5 |
| Expenditure on seeds | 133900 (31.6) | 135200 (32.0) | 153400 (36.3) | 422500 (100.0) |
| Average expenditure | 1300 | 1300 | 1300 | 1300.0 |
| Expenditure on fertilizers | 303850 (33.8) | 280800 (31.2) | 312700 (34.8) | 897350 (100.0) |
| Average expenditure | 2950 | 2700 | 2650 | 2761.0 |
| Expenditure on pesticides | 309000 (32.8) | 301600 (32.0) | 330400 (35.1) | 941000 (100.0) |
| Average expenditure | 3000 | 2900 | 2800 | 2895.3 |
| Expenditure on irrigation | 66950 (37.6) | 52000 (29.2) | 59000 (33.1) | 177950 (100.0) |
| Average expenditure | 650 | 500 | 500 | 547.5 |
| Expenditure on labour charges | 592250 (35.0) | 530400 (31.4) | 566400 (33.5) | 1689050 (100.0) |
| Average expenditure | 5750 | 5100 | 4800 | 5197.0 |
| **Total expenditure** | **1931250 (33.4)** | **1830400 (31.7)** | **2006000 (34.7)** | **5767650 (100.0)** |
| Average expenditure | 18750 | 17600 | 17000 | 17746.6 |

Source: Field study

Average expenditure per acre on commercial crops is worked out in the above table. Average for all crops per acre in study area is Rs. 17,746. However, there are variations ST and SC respondents have less than the average while BC respondents have more than the average expenditure. Unlike in the food crops SC respondents enjoy cost-benefit here along with ST respondents. Labour charges, cost of cultivation, fertilizers and pesticides are important items of expenditure. ST and SC respondents have an edge in labour costs over BC respondents.

**Table-2.22. Yield and Income particulars of the commercial crops**

| Caste | Area in acres | Total yield (qtl) | Average yield | Average price | Total income | Average income |
|---|---|---|---|---|---|---|
| BC | 103 (31.6) | 1345 (33.3) | 13.0 | 4000 | 5380000 (35.2) | 52233 |
| SC | 104 (32.0) | 1320 (32.7) | 12.6 | 3800 | 5016000 (32.8) | 48230 |
| ST | 118 (36.3) | 1370 (33.9) | 11.6 | 3560 | 4877200 (31.9) | 41332 |
| **Total** | **325 (100.0** | **4035 (100.0)** | **12.4** | **3786** | **15276510 (100.0)** | **47004** |

Source: Field study

Yield and income particulars from commercial crops are worked out in the above table. During this particular year of data collection prices are high along with yield. It is known fact that the prices of commercial crops are prone to steep changes in the market. As such per acre income is Rs, 47, 004 in the study area. BC respondents with progressive methods enjoy the maximum income of Rs. 52,233 per acre. BC respondents follow them. However, ST respondents have less than the average income per acre at Rs. 41,332 only. Incomes from commercial crops are akin to the incomes in gambling. As such they cannot sustain agriculture.

**Table-2.23. Efficiency particulars of food crops per acre**

| Caste | Area in acres | Total expen-diture | Average exp-enditure (per acre) | Total income | Average income (per acre) | Net income | Average net income |
|---|---|---|---|---|---|---|---|
| BC | 110 | 1666500 | 15150 | 2099000 | 19081 | 432500 | 3931 |

| | | | | | | | |
|---|---|---|---|---|---|---|---|
| | (40.1) | (45.0) | | (43.3) | | (38.0) | |
| SC | 84<br>(36.6) | 1139880<br>(30.7) | 13570 | 1494900<br>(30.8) | 17796 | 355020<br>(31.1) | 4226 |
| ST | 80<br>(29.1) | 896000<br>(24.2) | 11200 | 1261000<br>(26.0) | 15762 | 365000<br>(32.0) | 4562 |
| **Total** | **274<br>(100.0)** | **3702380<br>(100.0)** | **13512** | **4840274<br>(100.0)** | **17665** | **1137894<br>(100.0)** | **4152** |

Source: Field study

Efficiency particulars of the food crops per acre are examined in the above table. Efficiency quotients by taking of expenditure Rs. 1 of expenditure in relation to net income are calculated for their purpose. Average expenditure per acre in the study area is Rs. 13,512 while the average income for acre is Rs. 4152. The efficiency quotient is 1:0.31 in the study area. Caste wise, SC respondents have 1:0.41 as efficiency quotient. It implies that the net income is comfortable for these castes, being higher than the average SC respondents have 1:0.31 as quotient which equals the average. BC respondents are not comfortable as the quotient is 1:0.26 which is less than the average.

**Table-2.24. Efficiency particulars of commercial crops per acre**

| Caste | **Area in acres** | **Total expe-nditure** | **Average expen-diture (per acre)** | **Total income** | **Aver age inco me** | **Net income** | **Aver age net inco me** |
|---|---|---|---|---|---|---|---|
| BC | 103<br>(31.69) | 1931250<br>(33.4) | 18750 | 5380000<br>(35.2) | 5223<br>3 | 3448750<br>(36.2) | 3348<br>3 |
| SC | 104<br>(32.0) | 1830400<br>(31.7) | 17600 | 5016000<br>(32.8) | 4823<br>0 | 3185600<br>(33.5) | 3063<br>0 |
| ST | 118<br>(36.3) | 2006000<br>(34.7) | 17000 | 4877200<br>(31.9) | 4133<br>2 | 2871200<br>(30.1) | 2433<br>2 |
| **Total** | **325<br>(100.0)** | **5767650<br>(100.0)** | **17744** | **15276510<br>(100.0)** | **47004** | **9508860<br>(100.0)** | **29258** |

Source: Field study

Efficiency particulars of the commercial crops are analysed in the above table. Here also quotients are calculated caste wise and overall by adopting the earlier procedure. The overall efficiency quotient in the study area is 1:1.65 implying a net income Rs. 1.65 on every rupee spent on agriculture. It is very high and the limitations are discussed earlier. BC and SC respondents have 1:1.78 and 1:1.74 as efficiency quotients which are higher than the average quotient of the study area. ST respondents have below the average quotient of 1:1.44 implying lower net incomes is comparison with the other two castes.

**Table-2.25A. Average income particulars of the respondent families**

| Caste | Working population | Working size | Average for family member | Average total income for family | Annual Agri-culture income of family | Annual Non-agri-culture income of family |
|---|---|---|---|---|---|---|
| BC | 130 | 2.36 | 18484 | 48614 | 37414 | 11200 |
| SC | 165 | 2.89 | 15192 | 43906 | 34856 | 9050 |
| ST | 158 | 4.15 | 8769 | 36394 | 28894 | 7500 |
| **Total** | **453** | **3.02** | **14125** | **42660** | **33410** | **9250** |

Source: Field study

Income particular of the respondents are analysed in the above table. There are non- agricultural incomes to the respondents as most of them are small and marginal farmers. Total population is the study area is 670 and 453 (67.7%) are in the working age group. Family income, in the context, is a sum of agricultural and non-agricultural incomes. average income per family per annum is the study area is Rs. 42,660 of which Rs. 33,410 is agricultural and Rs. 9,250 is non-agricultural. However, BC and SC respondents have Rs. 48,614 and Rs. 43,906 as incomes which are higher than the average income. ST respondents have incomes which are less than the averages. Incomes of the BC respondents are higher in both agriculture and non-agriculture category. ST respondents are to be content with less than the average incomes of the study area in both categories.

**Table-2.26. Income and expenditure particulars of the respondent**

| Caste | Total population | Farm size | Average expenditure per year | Average total income per year | Average net income per year |
|---|---|---|---|---|---|
| BC | 170 | 3.0 | 23240 | 48614 | 25374 |
| SC | 240 | 4.2 | 21100 | 43906 | 22806 |
| ST | 260 | 6.8 | 19230 | 36394 | 17164 |
| **Total** | **670** | **4.4** | **21410** | **42660** | **21250** |

Source: Field study

Income and expenditure particulars, caste wise, are observed in the above table. To present a clear picture farm sizes of the respondents are also taken along with income and expenditure. Average net income in the study area per respondent is Rs. 42,660 against Rs. 21,410 as expenditure. Net income on an average per respondent is Rs. 21,250. Average farm size is 4.4 acres.

Farm size: Net income for the study area is Rs. 4829.5. Net income of the ST respondents is the lowest and the Farm size-Net Income Ratio is Rs. 2524. BC respondents are comfortable with net income of Rs. 25,374 and the ratio is Rs. 8458. SC respondents also have more than the average net income of the study area of Rs. 22,806 and the ratio is Rs. 5430. ST respondents are comparatively in receipt of low net incomes per acre.

**Table-2.27. Type of the residential houses of the respondents**

| Name of the Village | Name of the Mandal | Type of House | | | Total |
|---|---|---|---|---|---|
| | | Pucca | Semi-Pucca | Thatched | |
| Sthambampally | Geesukonda | 14 (20.5) | 8 (13.1) | 3 (14.2) | 25 (16.6) |
| Kommala | | 12 (17.6) | 10 (16.3) | 3 (14.2) | 25 (16.6) |
| Devannapeta | Hasanparthy | 12 (8.0) | 12 (19.7) | 1 (4.7) | 25 (16.6) |
| Chintagattu | | 11 (7.3) | 14 (22.9) | — | 25 (16.6) |

| Rajolu | Kuravi | 9 (6.0) | 10 (16.3) | 6 (28.5) | 25 (16.6) |
|---|---|---|---|---|---|
| Gundratimadugu | | 10 (14.7) | 7 (11.4) | 8 (38.0) | 25 (16.6) |
| **Total** | | **68 (45.3)** | **61 (40.7)** | **21 (14.0)** | **150 (100.0)** |

Source: Field study

There is any one thatched house in the Hasanparthy where SC are dominant. It implies that comfortable accommodation is limited. There are thatched houses even in the Geesugonda mandal where BCs are dominant.

**Table-2.28. Beneficiaries of the government housing programs**

| Name of the Village | Name of the Mandal | Nature of the House | | | | | | Total |
|---|---|---|---|---|---|---|---|---|
| | | BC | | SC | | ST | | |
| | | House | Site | House | Site | House | Site | |
| Stham-bampally | Geesu konda | 6 (27.2) | — | 8 (25.8) | 3 (23.0) | 3 (17.7) | 2 (10.0) | 22 (20.5) |
| Kommala | | 5 (22.7) | 1 (25.0) | 6 (19.3) | 1 (7.7) | 2 (11.7) | 3 (15.0) | 18 (16.8) |
| Devan-napeta | Hasanpar -thy | 4 (18.1) | — | 3 (9.6) | 2 (15.3) | 3 (17.6) | 1 (5.0) | 13 (12.1) |
| Chinta-gattu | | 3 (13.7) | — | 4 (12.9) | 1 (7.7) | 2 (11.7) | 3 (15.0) | 13 (12.1) |
| Rajolu | Kuravi | 2 (9.0) | 1 (25.0) | 6 (19.3) | 2 (15.3) | 3 (7.6) | 5 (25.0) | 19 (17.7) |
| Gundrati madugu | | 2 (9.0) | 2 (50.0) | 4 (12.9) | 4 (30.7) | 4 (23.5) | 6 (30.0) | 22 (20.5) |
| **Total** | | **22 (20.5)** | **4 (3.7)** | **31 (28.9)** | **13 (12.1)** | **17 (15.8)** | **20 (18.6)** | **107 (100.0)** |

Source: Field study

107 respondents are beneficiaries of the housing programs of the Government. 37 respondents are given house sites while 70 respondents are provided constructed houses. SC respondents are the maximum beneficiaries followed by ST and BC respondents.

**Table-2.29A.Assets of the respondent households**

| Name of the Village | Name of the Mandal | Assets | | | | | | | | | |
|---|---|---|---|---|---|---|---|---|---|---|---|
| | | Own house | Land | Bullock cart | Tractor | Oil engine | Bore well | T.V. | Two wheeler | Cell Phone | Bicycle |
| Sthambampally | Geesukonda | 22 (18.1) | 25 (16.6) | 8 (25.0) | 1 (14.2) | 8 (28.5) | 6 (20.7) | 20 (20.4 ) | 15 (21.7) | 21 (18.7) | 14 (13.8) |
| Kommala | | 20 (16.5) | 25 (16.6) | 9 (28.1) | 1 14.2) | 8 (28.5) | 8 (27.5) | 17 (17.3 ) | 11 (15.9) | 23 (20.5) | 13 (12.8) |
| Devannapeta | Hassanparthy | 21 (17.3) | 25 (16.6) | 2 (6.2) | 2 (28.5) | 3 (10.7) | 3 (10.3) | 16 (16.3 ) | 14 (20.2) | 18 (16.0) | 15 (14.8) |
| Chintagattu | | 22 (18.1) | 25 (16.6) | 3 (9.3) | 1 (14.2) | 4 (14.2) | 4 (13.7) | 23 (23.4 ) | 12 (17.3) | 21 (18.7) | 14 (13.8) |
| Rajolu | Kuravi | 19 (15.7) | 25 (16.6) | 4 (12.5) | 1 (14.2) | 7 (25.0) | 3 (10.3) | 14 (14.2 ) | 8 (11.3) | 16 (14.2) | 23 (22.7) |
| Gundrati madugu | | 17 (14.0) | 25 (16.6) | 6 (18.7) | 1 (14.2) | 8 (28.5) | 5 (17.2) | 8 (8.1) | 9 (13.0) | 13 (11.6) | 22 (21.7) |
| Total | | 121 (100.0) | 150 (100.0) | 32 (100.0) | 7 (100.0) | 28 (100.0) | 29 (100.0) | 98 (100.0) | 69 (100.0) | 112 (100.0) | 101 (100.0) |

Source: Field study

10 selected assets of the respondent households are estimated to identify the financial status. 10 items are taken as assets as given in the above table. All the respondents have land for cultivation with varying extents. 121 respondents have own houses. 112 respondents have cell phones, 101 respondents have bicycles, 98 respondents have tractors, 69 respondents have two wheelers, 32 respondents have bullock carts, 28 oil engines and 29 bore wells only 7 respondents have tractors assets are widely distributed. ST households have less number of T.Vs and cell phones. Even in housing they are less in numbers.

## B. Khammam District

Socio-Economic conditions of the respondent's six sample villages, two each from three mandals of Khammam District, the second unit of the sample are examined here. As mentioned already, in the summary of their chapter, a comparative analysis is given to estimate the similarities or otherwise.

**Table 2-30. Caste-wise particulars of the Respondents**

| Name of the Village | Name of the Manadal | BC | SC | ST | Total |
|---|---|---|---|---|---|
| Usirikayalapally | Karepally | 16 (34.7) | 04 (7.2) | 05 (10.2) | 25 (16.66) |
| Seetharampur | | 18 (39.1) | 04 (7.2) | 03 (6.1) | 25 (16.66) |
| Bodu | Tekulapally | 03 (6.5) | 06 (10.9) | 16 (32.6) | 25 (16.66) |
| Koppurai | | 01 (2.1) | 06 (10.9) | 18 (36.7) | 25 (16.66) |
| Thutikunta | Bonakal | 05 (10.8) | 15 (27.2) | 05 (10.2) | 25 (16.66) |
| Laxmipuram | | 03 (6.5) | 20 (36.3) | 02 (4.0) | 25 (16.66) |
| **Total** | | **46 (30.66)** | **55 (36.66)** | **49 (32.66)** | **150 (100.00)** |

Source: Field Study

Caste wise particulars of the respondents from the three mandals of the Khammam District as examined in the above table indicate that 46 are BCs, 55 are SCs and the remaining are STs. Karepally is a BC mandal while Tekulapally and Bonakal Mandals are of ST and SCs domination. The mandals are also selected to represent the three weaker sections. There is inter mix of castes in all the three mandals despite the domination of one caste. In all 150respondents are taken from Khammam district.

**Table-2.31. Caste-wise age Particulars of the Respondents**

| Caste | 20-30 | 30-40 | 40-50 | 50-60 | Above 60 | Total |
|---|---|---|---|---|---|---|
| BC | 02 (22.2) | 08 (30.7) | 2 (45.6) | 13 (22.8) | 02 (16.6) | 46 (30.33) |
| SC | 03 (33.3) | 12 (46.1) | 14 (30.4) | 24 (42.1) | 02 (16.6) | 55 (36.33) |
| ST | 04 (44.4) | 06 (23.7) | 11 (23.9) | 20 (35.0) | 08 (66.6) | 49 (32.33) |
| Total | 09 (6.00) | 26 (17.33) | 46 30.66) | 57 (38.00) | 12 (8.00) | 150 (100.00) |

Source: Field Study

Caste, age wise particulars of the respondents are observed. Most of the respondents 129 are in the 30-60 age group it is a welcome feature of the active age group is capable of taking up agriculture. It also shows that below 30 years age group engaged in non-agricultural activities. Only 12 (8%) respondents are above 60 years while 9 (6%) respondents are below 30 years of age.

**Table-2.32. Caste-wise literacy particulars of the respondents.**

| Caste | Literates | Illiterates | Total |
|---|---|---|---|
| BC | 20 (43.47) | 26 (25.0) | 46 (30.66) |
| SC | 15 (32.60) | 40 (38.46) | 55 (36.67) |
| ST | 11 (23.91) | 38 (36.53) | 49 (32.66) |
| **Total** | **46 (30.66)** | **104 (69.33)** | **150 (100.00)** |

Source: Field Study

104 (69.33%) respondents are illiterates. The futility of the compulsory education is well established by the data. 20 (44%) BC respondents are literates while 15 (37.5%) SC and 11 (22.5%) ST respondents are literates. In no caste literacy is at least 50%. This state of affairs exists in a district which is known for its awakening, awareness and consciousness. Agriculture cannot be progressive with dynamic changes as long as it is pursued by dull and docile human resource.

**Table-2.33. Caste-wise Education levels of the respondents**

| Caste | Primary | Secondary | Higher secondary | Total |
|---|---|---|---|---|
| BC | 14 (40.0) | 04 (50.0) | 02 (66.7) | 20 (43.4) |
| SC | 11 (31.4) | 03 (37.5) | 01 (33.3) | 15 (32.6) |
| ST | 10 (28.5) | 01 (12.5) | -(0.00) | 11 (23.9) |
| **Total** | **35 (76.08)** | **08 (17.39)** | **08 (17.39)** | **46 (100.0)** |

Source: Field Study

Education levels of the respondents are observed in above table of the 46 literates respondents. 35 (76.08) have completed primary education only.08 (17.39) respondents each have completed secondary and higher secondary education. No respondents from ST caste has completed higher secondary. Even among SCs and BCs only one and two respondents are with higher secondary education. B.C respondents are comparatively better in the levels of education.

**Table-2.34. School going children of the respondent households**

| Name of the village | Name of the Mandal | School Going Children | | | |
|---|---|---|---|---|---|
| | | **BC** | **SC** | **ST** | **Total** |
| Userikayalapally | Karepally | 16 (22.5) | 12 (20.7) | 10 (23.8) | 38 (22.2) |
| Setharampur | | 13 (18.3) | 08 (13.7) | 07 (16.7) | 28 (16.3) |
| Bodu | Tekulapally | 11 (15.4) | 06 (10.3) | 06 (10.3) | 23 (13.4) |

| Koppurai | | 10<br>(4.0) | 09<br>(15.5) | 04<br>(9.5) | 23<br>(13.4) |
|---|---|---|---|---|---|
| Thutikunta | Bonakal | 12<br>(16.9) | 10<br>(17.2) | 07<br>(16.7) | 29<br>(16.9) |
| Laxmipuram | | 09<br>(12.7) | 13<br>(22.4) | 08<br>(19.0) | 30<br>(17.5) |
| **Total** | | **71<br>(41.5)** | **58<br>(33.9)** | **42<br>(24.5)** | **171<br>(100.0)** |

Source: Field Study

School going children in the study area are 171. BC children are 71 (41.5%) SC 58 (33.9) and ST children are 42 (24.5) children constitute 27.1% of the total population of 630 in the study area. BC respondents have more children followed by SC and ST respondents.

**Table-2.35. School Drop outs of the Respondent Households**

| Name of the Village | Name of the Mandal | School Drop-outs | | | Total |
|---|---|---|---|---|---|
| | | BC | SC | ST | |
| Usirikayalapalli | Karepally | 1<br>(11.1) | 2<br>(14.2) | 1<br>(5.8) | 4<br>(10.0) |
| Seetarampur | | — | 2<br>(14.2) | 2<br>(11.7) | 4<br>(10.0) |
| Bodu | Tekulapally | 2<br>(22.2) | 3<br>(21.4) | 4<br>(23.5) | 9<br>(22.5) |
| Koppurai | | 1<br>(11.1) | 4 | 6<br>(35.2) | 11<br>(27.5) |
| Thitkunt | Bonakal | 3<br>(33.3) | 2<br>(14.2) | 3<br>(17.2) | 8<br>(20.0) |
| Laxmipuram | | 2<br>(22.2) | 1<br>(7.1) | 1<br>(5.8) | 4<br>(10.0) |
| **Total** | | **9<br>(22.5)** | **14<br>(35.0)** | **17<br>(42.5)** | **40<br>(100.0)** |

Source: Field Study

School drop-out children in the study area are 40. It implies that 131 children continue school education. In percentage terms 23.3 per cent of children are drop-outs and they are more in ST households followed by SC and BCs.

**Table–2.36. Sex-Wise distribution of the Respondent Households**

| Name of the Village | Name of the Mandal | Sex-Wise distribution | | | | | | Total |
|---|---|---|---|---|---|---|---|---|
| | | BC | | SC | | ST | | |
| | | M | F | M | F | M | F | |
| Usirikay-alapalli | Karepally | 14 (33.3) | 2 (50.0) | 3 (6.8) | 1 (9.0) | 4 (10.5) | 1 (9.0 | 25 (16.6) |
| Seetara-mpur | | 18 (42.8) | ___ | 4 (9.0) | ___ | 2 (5.2) | 1 (9.0) | 25 (16.6) |
| Bodu | Tekulapally | 2 (4.7) | 1 (25.0) | 5 (11.3) | 1 (9.0) | ) (26.3) | 6 (54.5 | 25 (16.6) |
| Koppurai | | 1 (2.3) | ___ | 4 (9.0) | 2 (18.0) | 5 (42.1) | (18.0) | 25 (16.6) |
| Thitkunt | Bonakal | 4 (9.5) | 1 (25.0) | 0 (22.7) | 5 (45.4) | 4 (10.5) | 1 (9.0) | 25 (16.6) |
| Laxmi-puram | | 3 (7.1) | ___ | 18 (40.9) | 2 (18.0) | 2 (5.2) | ___ | 25 (16.6) |
| **Total** | | **42 (28.0** | **4 (2.7)** | **44 (29.3)** | **11 (7.3** | **8 (25.3)** | **11 (7.3)** | **150 (100.0)** |

Source: Field Study

26 respondents are females and the remaining 126 are males. Female respondents are more among ST and SC. Only 4 are females from the BC caste. In terms of percentage females are 17.3.

**Table-2.37. Caste-wise type of the family**

| Caste | Joint | Nuclear | Total |
|---|---|---|---|
| BC | 18 (33.3) | 28 (29.1) | 46 (30.66) |
| SC | 21 (38.8) | 34 (35.4) | 55 (36.66) |
| ST | 15 (27.7) | 34 (35.4) | 49 (32.66) |
| **Total** | **54 (36.0)** | **96 (64.0)** | **150 (100.0)** |

Source: Field Study

It is noted that most of the respondents 96(64%) are in Nuclear families confining to the modern trend. It does not mean that traditional joint families are totally given up. It is noteworthy that 54 (36%) respondents are in the joint families. One of the basic reasons for preferring joint families in the rural

India may be the need of more labour in Agriculture. 21 (40%) SC respondents are in joint families against 21 (35%) BC and 15(31%) ST respondents. More SC respondents are in favour of joint families.

**Table-2.38. Caste-wise occupational particulars of the respondents**

| Caste | Agriculture | Non-agriculture (AL) | Total |
|---|---|---|---|
| BC | 28 (22.0) | 18 (78.2) | 46 (30.66) |
| SC | 52 (40.9) | 03 (13.0) | 55 (36.67) |
| ST | 47 (37.0) | 02 (8.6) | 49 (32.66) |
| **Total** | **127 (84.7)** | **23 (15.3)** | **150 (100.00)** |

Source: Field Study

127 (84.7%) respondents are agriculturists while the remaining 23 (15.3%) respondents are agricultural labourers. Agricultural labourers have no land of any nature and their primary occupation is wage-work. 18 (78.2%) respondents under labour category are BCs. 3 and 2 respondents from SC and ST castes are pure labourers. It implies that some BC households in the rural areas have no land.

**Table-2.39. Caste-wise category particulars of the respondents**

| Name of the Village | M.F | S.F | Med.F | B.F | AL | Total |
|---|---|---|---|---|---|---|
| BC | 08 (27.58) | 17 (27.86) | 02 (6.6) | 01 (14.28) | 18 (78.2) | 46 (30.66) |
| SC | 13 (44.82) | 32 (52.45) | 05 (16.66) | 02 (28.57) | 03 (13.0) | 55 (36.66) |
| ST | 08 (27.58) | 12 (19.67) | 23 (76.66) | 04 (57.14) | 02 (8.6) | 49 (32.66) |
| Total | 29 (22.83) | 61 (48.03) | 30 (23.62) | 07 (5.51) | 23 (15.3) | 150 (100.0) |

Source: Field Study

Respondents are classified into categories based on the land under their disposal. 23 respondents have no land and remain as pure labourers. Marginal farmers are 29 (22.83%), small farmers 61 (48.03%), medium farmers 30 (23.62%) and big farmers are 7 (5.51%). Data in table 7 clearly states that 90 (70.86%) respondents are either marginal or small farmers implying the small size of agricultural holdings. Big farmers are just seven. More ST respondents 4 are in this category. ST respondents are more 23 among medium farmers also which indicate that ST respondents have comparatively large holdings. Only 20 ST respondents are among small and marginal categories of the 46 BC respondents only 3 are in the medium and big farmers' categories. 18 are agricultural labourers only while 25 respondents are in the marginal and small farmers categories. Only 7 SC respondents are in the medium and big farmers categories while the remaining. 48 are in the marginal and small farmers categories with 3 labourers. The data states that STs respondents are comfortable in the process of cultivation. Even among the ST respondents 2 are agricultural labourers.

**Table–2.40. Land particulars of the respondents**

| Caste | Own | Leased | Both | Total |
|---|---|---|---|---|
| BC | 24 (26.96) | 02 (8.33) | 02 (14.28) | 28 (22.04) |
| SC | 30 (33.70) | 15 (62.5) | 07 (50.00) | 52 (40.94) |
| ST | 35 (39.32) | 07 (29.16) | 05 (35.71) | 47 (37.07) |
| **Total** | **89 (70.07)** | **24 (18.89)** | **14 (11.02)** | **127 (100.00)** |

Source: Field Study

It is noted from the data in the above table that 89 respondents have own land. 14 respondents have both own and leased lands. Together 103 out of 127 respondents have own land irrespective of the extent. In other words 81.09% of the respondents are owner-cultivators. Absentee landlordism is confined to 24 respondents only. This fact is also noteworthy as the owner-cultivator has inclination to develop land on regular and permanent basis.

**Table-2.41. Particulars of the land by the respondents**

| Caste | Wet land (in acres) | Dry land (in acres) | Total land (in acres) |
|---|---|---|---|
| BC | 45 (15.2) | 101 (25.5) | 146 (21.12) |
| SC | 139 (46.9) | 70 (17.7) | 209 (30.24) |
| ST | 112 (37.8) | 224 (56.7) | 336 (48.62) |
| **Total** | **296 (42.83)** | **395 (57.16)** | **691 (100.00)** |

Source: Field Study

127 respondents from this study unit are cultivators and the total land cultivated is 691 acres as given in the above table. 296 (42.83%) acres are wet whereas 395 (57.16%) acres are dry. Dry land, in terms of area, is more land 336 (48.62%) acres followed by SC 209 (30.24%) and BC 140 (21.12%) acres respectively. It is clear that the dominant caste in land ownership is ST since Khammam district has the maximum ST population. SC respondents have more wet land whereas ST and BC respondents have more dry land.

**Table-2.42. Particulars of irrigation facilities**

| Caste | Yes | No | Total |
|---|---|---|---|
| BC | 10 (16.9) | 18 (26.4) | 28 (22.4) |
| SC | 37 (62.7) | 15 (22.0) | 52 (40.94) |
| ST | 12 (20.3) | 35 (51.4) | 47 (37.07) |
| **Total** | **59 (46.45)** | **68 (53.54)** | **127 (100.00)** |

Source: Field Study

59 (46.45%) respondents have irrigation facilities against 68 (53.55%) respondents with no such facility SC respondents are lucky to enjoy more irrigation facilities. 71% of the SC respondents enjoy their facility whereas it available to 34% of BC and 26% of ST respondents. ST respondents, mostly carry on agriculture with limited or little irrigation facilities.

**Table-2.43. Particulars of source-wise irrigation**

| Caste | Canal | Tanks | Open wells | Bore wells | More than one | Total |
|---|---|---|---|---|---|---|
| BC | - (00.0) | 06 (27.27) | 02 (40.0) | 01 (100.0) | 01 (33.3) | 10 (16.94) |
| SC | 28 (100.0) | 07 (31.81) | - (00.0) | - (00.0) | 02 (66.6) | 37 (62.71) |
| ST | - (00.0) | 09 (40.90) | 03 (60.0) | - (00.0) | - (00.0) | 12 (20.33) |
| **Total** | **28 (47.45)** | **22 (37.28)** | **05 (8.47)** | **01 (16.94)** | **03 (5.08)** | **59 (100.00)** |

Source: Field Study

Canals and tanks together are the two most important sources of irrigation benefiting 75% of the respondents with irrigation facilities. Open wells and bore wells help just six while 3 respondents depend on more than one source. As mentioned earlier SC respondents 37 are the maximum beneficiaries while 10 BC respondents and 12 SC respondents depend on other than canal sources.

**Table-2.44. Means of irrigation by the respondents**

| Caste | Electrical motors | Direct canal | Total |
|---|---|---|---|
| BC | 04 (25.0) | 06 (13.9) | 10 (16.94) |
| SC | 09 (56.2) | 28 (65.1) | 37 (62.71) |
| ST | 03 (18.7) | 09 (20.9) | 12 (20.33) |
| **Total** | **16 (27.11)** | **43 (72.88)** | **59 (100.00)** |

Source: Field Study

Only 16 respondents use electrical motors and 9 of them are SCs. Respondents from the other two castes are 4 BC and 3 STs only. Most of the SC respondents 28 get direct canal water which is cost effective, only 9 (ST) and 6 (BC) respondents have accession to direct canal water as observed from the above table.

**Table-2.45. Crop-wise particulars of the respondents (In acres)**

| Crops | BC | SC | ST | Total |
|---|---|---|---|---|
| Paddy | 09 (32.1) | 14 (26.9) | 13 (27.6) | 36 (28.34) |
| Cotton | 08 (28.5) | 13 (25.0) | 10 (21.2) | 31 (24.40) |
| Both | 05 (17.8) | 21 (40.38) | 19 (40.4) | 45 (35.43) |
| Mize | 03 (10.7) | 02 (3.8) | 03 (6.3) | 08 (6.21) |
| Red gram | 02 (7.1) | - (00.0) | 01 (2.1) | 03 (2.36) |
| Chilly | 01 (3.5) | 02 (3.8) | - (00.0) | 03 (2.36) |
| Black gram | - (00.0) | - (00.0) | 01 (2.1) | 01 (0.78) |
| **Total** | **28 (22.04)** | **52 (40.94)** | **47 (37.07)** | **127 (100.00)** |

Source: Field Study

Crop pattern in the study area is analysed in the above table. Cotton and Paddy crops are cultivated by 112 respondents. 88% of the respondents prefer these crops. Only 8 respondents grow maize and other crops are not significant. Cotton and Paddy are mostly favoured by all the respondents. Maize crop is opted by very few and the other crops are of no importance.

**Table – 2.46. Particulars of crop-wise farm-size of the respondents**

| Caste | Crops | Paddy | Cotton | Mize | Red gram | Chilly | Black gram | Total |
|---|---|---|---|---|---|---|---|---|
| BC | Respo-ndents | 10 (35.7) | 12 (42.8) | 03 (10.7) | 02 (7.1) | 01 (3.1) | - (00.0) | 28 (100.0) |
| | Area | 45 (31.0) | 92 (63.0) | 06 (4.1) | 01 (0.6) | 02 (1.3) | (00.0) | 146 (100.0) |
| | Farm-size | 4.5 | 7.6 | 2.0 | 0.5 | 2.0 | (00.0) | 5.2 |
| SC | Resp-ondents | 19 (36.5) | 18 (34.7) | 10 (9.2) | 01 (1.9) | 03 (5.7) | 01 (1.9) | 52 (100.0) |
| | Area | 132 (63.1) | 43 (20.5) | 25 (11.9) | 01 (0.4) | 07 (3.3) | 01 (0.4) | 209 (100.0) |
| | Farm-size | 6.9 | 2.2 | 2.5 | 1.0 | 2.3 | 1.0 | 4.1 |
| ST | Res-pondents | 15 (31.9) | 21 (44.6) | 08 (17.0) | 01 (2.1) | (00.0) | 02 (4.2) | 47 (100.0) |
| | Area | 108 (32.1) | 204 (60.8) | 21 (6.2) | 02 (0.6) | (00.0) | 01 (0.3) | 336 (100.0) |
| | Farm-size | 7.2 | 9.7 | 2.6 | 2.0 | (00.0) | 0.5 | 7.1 |

| Total | Respondents | 44 (34.7) | 52 (40.1) | 21 (16.5) | 03 (2.3) | 04 (3.1) | 03 (2.3) | 127 (100.0) |
|---|---|---|---|---|---|---|---|---|
| | Area | 285 (41.2) | 339 (49.0) | 53 (7.6) | 03 (0.4) | 09 (1.3) | 02 (0.2) | 691 (100.0) |
| | Farm-size | 6.4 | 6.5 | 2.5 | 1.1 | 2.2 | 0.7 | 5.4 |

Source: Field Study

Farm size under different crops, caste wise is worked out in above table to estimate the variations. These are 691 acres under the disposal of 127 respondents is the study area. Average farm size for the study area is 5.4 acres. However, ST respondents have big farmers 7.1 acres while BC and SC respondents possess 5.2 acres and 4.1 acres respectively. In other words farm sizes of BC and SC respondents are less than the average for the study area. These variations are reflected in the farm sizes under different crops. 90% of the total land is under Paddy and Cotton crops and the farm sizes are 6.4 and 6.5 acres respectively. However, SC and ST respondents have more than the average size under paddy. Coming to cotton SC respondents have just 2.2 acres whereas the other two castes have larger farms then the average.

**Table-2.47. Particulars of farm-size under food and commercial corps (in acres)**

| Crops | Food crops | | | Commercial crops | | |
|---|---|---|---|---|---|---|
| **Caste** | **Respondents** | **Area** | **Farm-size** | **Respondents** | **Area** | **Farm-size** |
| BC | 15 (21.7) | 52 (15.2) | 3.46 | 13 (22.4) | 94 (26.8) | 7.23 |
| SC | 30 (43.40 | 158 (46.3) | 5.26 | 22 (37.9) | 51 (14.5) | 2.21 |
| ST | 24 (34.7) | 131 (38.4) | 5.45 | 23 (39.6) | 205 (58.5) | 9.31 |
| **Total** | **69 (100.0)** | **341 (100.0)** | **4.94** | **58 (100.0)** | **350 (100.0)** | **6.03** |
| | 127 | | | 127 | | |

Source: Field Study

Land allocation to food crops and commercial crops is very close. 341 acres are under food crops against 350 acres are under commercial crops. Average farm size under food crops is 4.94 acres whereas average under the commercial crops is 6.03 acres. There are variations here also. ST and SC respondents have higher sizes than the average in food crops while BC respondents have less than the average farm size. With regard to commercial crops, again ST respondents have bigger farms than the average size along with BC respondents. The table reveals that the ST respondents have bigger farms in both food and commercial crops.

**Table-2.48. Average expenditure on food crops per acre**

| Caste | BC | SC | ST | Total |
|---|---|---|---|---|
| Area in acres | 52 (15.2) | 158 (46.3) | 131 (38.4) | 341 (100.0) |
| Exp. on cultivation | 166400 (16.1) | 481900 (46.8) | 379900 (36.9) | 1028200 (100.0) |
| Average exp. | 3200 | 3050 | 2900 | 3015.24 |
| Exp. on seeds | 31300 (15.3) | 93220 (46.1) | 77290 (38.3) | 201810 (100.0) |
| Average exp. | 601 | 590 | 590 | 591.8 |
| Exp. on fertilizer | 135720 (16.7) | 347600 (42.9) | 328810 (40.6) | 809130 (100.0) |
| Average exp. | 2610 | 2200 | 2510 | 2372.8 |
| Exp. on pesticides | 37440 (17.0) | 103490 (47.1) | 78600 (35.8) | 219530 (100.0) |
| Average exp. | 720 | 655 | . 600 | 643.7 |
| Exp. on irrigation | 44200 (24.1) | 86900 (47.4) | 52007 (28.4) | 183107 (100.0) |
| Average exp. | 850 | 550 | 397 | 536.9 |
| Exp. on labou charges | 257400 (15.6) | 761560 (46.1) | 630110 (38.2) | 1649070 (100.0) |
| Average exp. | 4950 | 4820 | 4810 | 4835.9 |
| **Total exp.** | **672460** | **1874670** | **1546717** | **4093847** |
| Average exp. | 12931 | 11865 | 11807 | 12005.4 |

Source: Field Study

Average expenditure on food crops per acre is calculated item wise as given in the above table. Average expenditure in the study area on the food crops per acre is Rs.12,005. However, cost of cultivation is not uniform. SCs spend Rs. 11,865 per acre whereas ST respondents spend Rs.11,807. It implies that these two castes have cost effectiveness. Cost of cultivation per acre with regard to BCs is more than the average in the study area at Rs. 12,931. Expenditure on plowing and other operations together with fertilizer and labour charges are the important components of the costs. Seeds, pesticides and irrigation charges are not so important.

**Table – 2.49. Yield and income particulars of food crops**

| Caste | Area in acres | Total yield (qtl) | Average yield (qtl) | Average price | Total income | Average income |
|---|---|---|---|---|---|---|
| BC | 52 (15.2) | 910 (17.1) | 17.5 | 980 | 891800 (17.2) | 17150 |
| SC | 158 (46.3) | 2528 (47.5) | 16.0 | 1015 | 2565920 (49.4) | 16240 |
| ST | 131 (38.4) | 1874 (35.2) | 14.3 | 935 | 1752190 (33.7) | 13375 |
| **Total** | **341 (100.0)** | **5312 (100.0)** | **15.5** | **976** | **5184512 (100.0)** | **15203** |

Source: Field Study

Yield and income particulars of food crops are estimated in the above table. Yield in quintals is multiplied by the prevailing price to arrive at incomes. Average income per acre in the study area is Rs 15,203. However, BC respondents with per acre average income of Rs. 17,150 and SC respondents with Rs. 16,240 per acre have more than the average income. They have edge over ST respondents whose average income is less than the average in the study area of at Rs. 13,375. ST respondents are not deriving higher incomes.

**Table- 2.50. Average expenditure on commercial crops per acre**

| Caste | BC | SC | ST | Total |
|---|---|---|---|---|
| Area in acres | 94 (26.8) | 51 (14.5) | 205 (58.5) | 350 (100.0) |
| Expenditure on cultivation | 321480 (28.8) | 159630 (14.3) | 633450 (56.8) | 1114560 (100.0) |
| Average expenditure | 3420 | 3130 | 3090 | 3184.45 |
| Expenditure on seeds | 74260 (28.3) | 38250 (14.6) | 149650 (57.0) | 262160 (100.0) |
| Average expenditure | 790 | 750 | 730 | 749.02 |
| Expenditure on fertilizers | 253800 (27.5) | 132855 (14.4) | 535050 (58.0) | 921705 (100.0) |
| Average expenditure | 2700 | 2605 | 2610 | 2633.44 |
| Expenditure on pesticides | 211500 (28.7) | 107100 (14.5) | 416150 (56.6) | 734750 (100.0) |
| Average expenditure | 2250 | 2100 | 2030 | 2099.2 |
| Expenditure on irrigation | 47000 (37.5) | 22950 (18.3) | 55350 (44.1) | 125300 (100.0) |
| Average expenditure | 500 | 450 | 270 | 358 |
| Expenditure on labour charges | 500080 (27.7) | 265710 (1.4) | 1035250 (57.4) | 1801040 (100.0) |
| Average expenditure | 5320 | 5210 | 5050 | 5145.82 |
| **Total expenditure** | **1408120 (29.8)** | **726495 (14.6)** | **2824900 (56.9)** | **4959515 (100.0)** |
| Average expenditure | 14980 | 14245 | 13780 | 14170 |

Source: Field Study

Average expenditure on commercial crops per acre is worked out and it is observed that the average is Rs. 14,170, slightly less than the average expenditure per acre on food crops.

Here also BC respondents incur Rs.14,980 has expenditure which is more than average in the study area. The average expenditure per acre by the SC respondents is also higher than the average in the study area at Rs.14,245. ST respondents have low cost of cultivation per acre at Rs. 13,780

**Table-2.51. Yield and income particulars of commercial crops (per acre)**

| Caste | Area in acres | Total yield (qtl) | Average yield (qtl) | Average price | Total income | Average income |
|---|---|---|---|---|---|---|
| BC | 94 (26.8) | 1129 (29.9) | 12.0 | 3250 | 3669250 (31.6) | 39034 |
| SC | 51 (14.5) | 587 (15.5) | 11.5 | 3000 | 1743000 (15.0) | 34176 |
| ST | 205 (58.5) | 2050 (54.4) | 10.0 | 3000 | 6150000 (52.9) | 30000 |
| **Total** | **350 (100.0)** | **3766 (100.0)** | **10.7** | **3083** | **11610578** | **33173** |

Source: Field Study

Yield and income particulars of commercial crops per acre in the study area are worked out in the above table. The same process for food crops is followed here also. Average income from commercial crops is Rs. 33,173, however they are variations in the caste wise overage incomes. BCs come first with Rs.39,034 followed SC respondents with Rs.34,176 and ST respondents are at the bottom with Rs. 30,000 per acre. Cost wise ST respondents are superior but income wise they are at the bottom. This interesting situation is because ST respondents have 205 acres (58.5) out of total of 350 acres of land. In other words land under control of ST respondents is more giving less scope for intensive cultivation. Average yield per acre of the ST respondents is the lowest 10 quintals against the average yield of 10.7 quintals in the study area.

**Table-2.52. Efficiency particulars of food crops (per acre)**

| Caste | Area in acres | Total Exp. | Average exp. | Total income | Average income | Net income | Average net income |
|---|---|---|---|---|---|---|---|
| BC | 52 (15.24) | 673460 (16.4) | 12931 | 891800 (17.2) | 17150 | 218340 (20.0) | 4198 |
| SC | 158 (40.3) | 1874670 (45.8) | 11865 | 2565920 (49.4) | 16240 | 691250 (63.3) | 4375 |
| ST | 131 (38.41) | 1546717 (37.7) | 11807 | 17521920 (33.7) | 13375 | 205473 (18.8) | 1568 |
| **Total** | **341 (100.0)** | **4093847 (100.0)** | **12005** | **5184512 (100.0)** | **15203** | **1090665 (100.0)** | **3198** |

Source: Field Study

Efficiency particulars of food crops are computed in the above table with the help of efficiency quotients. Efficiency quotients are worked out by dividing the average net income with the average expenditure. It shows the net income generated per an expenditure of Rs.01. Efficiency quotients for the study area for food crops is 1:0.27. BC and ST respondents are comfortable with higher quotients than the average quotients. ST respondents are losing behind in generating incomes. Any way the quotients indicate that cultivation of food crops is not so benefited as net incomes are not encouraging.

**Table-2.53. Efficiency particulars of commercial crops (per acre)**

| Caste | Area in acres | Total exp | Average exp. (per acre) | Total income | Average income (per acre) | Net income | Average net income |
|---|---|---|---|---|---|---|---|
| BC | 94 (26.85) | 1481020 (29.8) | 14980 | 3669250 (31.6) | 39034 | 2188230 (32.5) | 23279 |

| | | | | | | | |
|---|---|---|---|---|---|---|---|
| SC | 51 (14.5 | 726495 (14.6) | 14245 | 1743000 (15.0) | 34176 | 10165 05 (15.1) | 19931 |
| ST | 205 (58.5) | 28249 00 (56.9) | 13780 | 6150000 (52.9) | 30000 | 33251 00 (49.5) | 16220 |
| **Total** | **350 (100.0)** | **495951 (100.0** | **14170** | **11610578 (100.0)** | **33173** | **665106 (100.0** | **19003** |

Source: Field Study

Efficiency particulars of commercial crops per acre are worked out on the same lines followed for food crops. Interestingly, prices of the commercial crops are never stable. Steep up and down in prices are common in the market. Based on the market prices while collecting data by the researcher the figures are worked out. The average efficiency quotients for commercial crop in the study area are 1:1.34. It means that an in investment of 1 rupee net income is Rs.1.34. However, BCs with 1:1.55 quotients and SCs with 1:1.4 quotients are comfortable. Efficiency quotient of the ST respondents is the lowest. Even then they receive Rs.1.17 with an expenditure of 1 rupee. Incomes from commercial crops are like the earnings in a gimble. They are never certain and sustainable.

**Tabla-2.54. Average income particulars of the respondents family**

| Caste | Wor-king popu-lation | Working size | Average income for family member | Average total income | Agricultur e income per family per year | Non-agriculture income per family per year |
|---|---|---|---|---|---|---|
| BC | 73 | 1.5 | 28168 | 44507 | 27497 | 17010 |
| SC | 146 | 2.6 | 14500 | 38426 | 24306 | 14120 |
| ST | 191 | 3.8 | 7960 | 30988 | 17788 | 13200 |
| **Tota** | **410** | **2.7** | **13544** | **36977** | **22201** | **14776** |

Source: Field Study

Average incomes of the respondent families are examined in the above table. Average income in the study area per annum is Rs.14,776. They are disparities in thee caste wise incomes. BC respondents have Rs.17,010 per family an average and they at the top. SC respondents an average have Rs.14,120 per family per year. ST respondents have Rs.13,200 per family per year and they at the bottom. Both the SC and ST respondents have the average incomes which are less than the average in the study area. Working age group in the study area is 410 (65.0%). Size of the working group is more among the ST respondents followed by SC (2.6%) and BC (1.5%) respondents. The average size of the working group in the study is 2.7 per cent.

**Table-2.55. Income and expenditure particulars of the respondents**

| Caste | Total population | Family size | Average total expenditure per year | Average total income per year | Average net income per year |
|---|---|---|---|---|---|
| BC | 125 | 2.7 | 22126 | 44507 | 22381 |
| SC | 209 | 3.8 | 18330 | 38426 | 20096 |
| ST | 296 | 6.0 | 17130 | 30988 | 13858 |
| **Total** | **630** | **4.2** | **19101** | **36977** | **17876** |

Source: Field Study

However, BCs and SCs have more than the average surplus whereas STs have less than the average. Averages by themselves cannot indicate that all the respondents have surplus. They give a rough picture only.

**Table-2.56. Type of the residential houses of the Respondent Households**

| Name of the Village | Name of the Mandal | Type of House | | | Total |
|---|---|---|---|---|---|
| | | Pucca | Semi-Pucca | Thatched | |
| Usirikayalapalli | Karepally | 16<br>(30.1) | 6<br>(9.0) | 3<br>(9.6) | 25<br>(16.6) |
| Seetarampur | | 13<br>(24.5) | 10<br>(15.1) | 2<br>(6.4) | 25<br>(16.6) |
| Bodu | Tekulapally | 4 | 12 | 9 | 25 |

| | | | | | |
|---|---|---|---|---|---|
| | | (7.5) | (18.0) | (29.0) | (16.6) |
| Koppurai | | 1 (1.8) | 17 (25.7) | 7 (22.5) | 25 (16.6) |
| Thitkunt | Bonakal | 8 (15.0) | 13 (19.6) | 4 (12.9) | 25 (16.6) |
| Laxmipuram | | 11 (20.7) | 8 (12.1) | 6 (19.3) | 25 (16.6) |
| **Total** | | **53 (35.3)** | **66 (44.0)** | **31 (20.7)** | **150 (100.0)** |

Source: Field Study

All the 150 respondents have residential houses. 31 (20.7) respondents are in thatched houses even today. ST respondents are more (16) in thatched houses followed by SC and BC respondents. BC respondents are more comfortable in housing facilities.

**Table – 2.57. Beneficiaries of the Government housing programs**

| Name of the Village | Name of the Mandal | Nature of the Benefit | | | | | | Total |
|---|---|---|---|---|---|---|---|---|
| | | BC | | SC | | ST | | |
| | | House | Site | House | Site | House | Site | |
| Usirikaya-lapalli | Kare-pally | 7 (36.8) | 3 (60.0) | 2 (6.7) | 2 (18.1) | 3 (12.5) | ___ | 17 (16.5) |
| Seetarampur | | 6 (31.5) | ___ | 3 (10.0) | 1 (9.0) | 2 (8.3) | 1 (7.1) | 13 (12.7) |
| Bodu | Tekul-apally | 2 (10.5) | 1 (20.0) | 4 (13.3) | ___ | 8 (33.3) | 3 (21.4) | 18 (17.4) |
| Koppurai | | ___ | ___ | 2 (6.7) | 1 (9.0) | 5 (20.8) | 10 (71.4) | 18 (17.4) |
| Thitkunt | Bona-kal | 3 (15.7) | 1 (20.0) | 8 (26.7) | 3 (27.2) | 4 (16.7) | ___ | 19 (18.4) |
| Laxmipuram | | 1 (5.2) | ___ | 11 (36.7) | 4 (36.3) | 2 (8.3) | ___ | 18 (17.4) |
| **Total** | | **19 (18.4)** | **5 (4.8)** | **30 (29.1)** | **11 (10.7)** | **24 (23.3)** | **14 (13.5)** | **103 (100.0)** |

Source: Field Study

103 respondents are beneficiaries of the Government housing programmes. 30 respondents have received house sites while the remaining 73 have received houses. Maximum beneficiaries are SCs followed by ST and BC respondents.

## Summary

Socio-economic conditions in the study area are analysed in this chapter. The study covers 150 respondents each from Warangal and Khammam districts. In order to establish similarities or otherwise analysis is made separately for each district. The two districts are contiguous geographically.

Weaker sections of the rural area viz., BC, SC and ST castes are taken for this study. Each mandal is dominated by a particular caste population wise. In other words the three castes chosen represent the three mandal in each district. Most of the respondents in both districts are below 60 years of age and so age experience are in favour of the respondents to face the strain of agriculture. Literacy is identical in both the districts. However, illiteracy is more in the mandals of Khammam district. Literacy among the BCs is the highest and STs in both areas are mostly illiterate. Most of the respondents have completed only primary education. School going children are 27.6 per cent of the total family members of the respondent households in Warangal district whereas in Khammam district they are 24.5. School drop-outs are more among ST children. School drop-outs in the study area of Khammam are 19 against 40 in Warangal districts. Drop-outs are less among BC children. Nuclear families are popular in both districts. However, more than 1/3rd of the respondents area in the joint families. 26 respondents are females in Khammam district whereas 23 are females in Warangal district. Female respondents are among ST and SC families. 31 respondents in Khammam district and 21 in

Warangal district of the study area reside in thatched houses. Government housing programmes have helped the respondents to possess living accommodation. All the respondents in Warangal district depend on agriculture as main occupation while 127 respondents depend on agriculture in Khammam district. 23 respondents take up both agricultural and non-agricultural activities as casual labourers. Medium and big farmers are more in Khammam district than in Warangal district. Marginal farmers are more in Warangal district. In both areas small and marginal farmers put together are dominant in number. Land leasing and rent payments are common in both the districts indicating absentee landlordism to some extent.57.16 per cent of land in Khammam district is dry while 43.7 per cent of land is dry in Warangal district. Dominant caste in land ownership in Khammam district is STs whereas in Warangal district BCs have more land at their disposal. Irrigation facilities are more in Warangal districts. Canals and open wells are important in Warangal district as irrigation sources while canals and tanks are important in Khammam district. Electrical motors are used more in Warangal district. Cotton and Paddy crops are preferred by the respondents in both areas. Chillies for which the two district are popular are cultivated to some extent. Average farm size is 5.4 acres in Khammam district, whereas it is 3.9 acres in Warangal district. There are variations in the farm size from caste to caste and from crop to crop. Land allocation to food crops and commercial crops is very close in Khammam district. However, more land is allocated to commercial crops in Warangal district. Average expenditure on food crops per acre in Warangal district is higher Rs. 13,512.3 than that of Khammam districts which is Rs.12,005.4. Here also there are variations from caste to caste. STs and SCs have cost effectively. Average income per acre from food crops in Warangal Rs.17,665 against Rs. 15,203 in Khammam district. ST respondents in both districts have low per acre incomes from food crops. Average expenditure on commercial crops is higher Rs.17,746.6 in Warangal district when compared to Rs.14,170 of Khammam districts. Cost of cultivation of both food and commercial crops is comparatively higher in Warangal district. Average income per acre from commercial crops is high in both districts. Respondents in Warangal district get Rs. 47,004 per acre while respondents in Khammam district receive Rs. 33,173. In both districts per acre incomes of the ST respondents are the lowest. Efficiency quotient for food crops is 1:0.27 in Khammam district whereas it is 1:0.31 inn Warangal district. Quotient for commercial crops are 1:1.34 in Khammam district against 1:1.65 in Warangal district. It clearly shows that commercial crops are more remunerative and slowly food crops are given holidays. Average income per annum in Khammam district is Rs. 36,977 whereas the average income in Warangal district is Rs. 42,660. Average expenditure for family in Khammam district is Rs.19,101 against Rs. 21,410 in Warangal district. 10 selected assets to estimate the relative positions of the respondents are analysed. Own houses and land ownership are widely distributed. However, ST respondents in both districts of the study area are in a disadvantageous position.

Economic activities are guided, motivated and directed by the socio-economic conditions. Similarities are there between the two districts in some basic factors. At the same time variations, too, exist.

# 3

# Utilisation of Credit and Implications of Rural Indebtedness

In the preceding chapter Rural Indebtedness has been analysed and established. This chapter deals with credit utilisation by the respondents by following the same procedure of the chapter-III in the tables. Credit, if used effectively, can generate additional incomes with which the outstanding loans can be cleared. But the socio-economic conditions of the weaker sections in the rural area are fraught with uncertainty. They have so many unexpected commitments for which they have to divert the borrowed amounts. Most of these commitments are unproductive. Indebtedness goes on increasing. The weaker sections are driven in to the vicious circle of poverty and indebtedness from which escape becomes a mirage. They suffer and groan under the burden of indebtedness. Their overall life is effected due to indebtedness. The implications of indebtedness are also analysed in this chapter to estimate the condition of living of the indebted households.

Institutional agencies demand documents and acceptable securities. Most of the respondents are illiterate. They have to spend on middle men and they cannot directly speak to the authorities. So they face problems in taking loans from the institutional agencies. The basic problem in taking loans from institutional agencies are elaborated in the following table.

**Table-3.1. Problems in taking loans from the institutional agencies**

| Caste | Delay in sanc-tioning | Middle men | Unfavoura ble terms of repayment | Difficulty in Document ation | Total |
|---|---|---|---|---|---|
| BC | 18+15=33 (32.6) | 4+2=6 (20.0) | 16+13=29 (37.6) | 17+16=33 (35.8) | 55+46 =101 (33.7) |
| SC | 21+18=39 (38.6) | 8+6=14 (46.6) | 17+10=27 (35.0) | 11+21=33 (35.8) | 57+55 =112 (37.3) |
| ST | 16+13=29 (28.7) | 6+4=10 (33.3) | 12+9=21 (27.2) | 4+23=27 (29.3) | 38+49 =87 (29.0) |
| **Total** | **55+46 =101 (33.7)** | **18+12= 30 (10.0)** | **45+32=77 (25.6)** | **32+60=92 (30.6)** | **150+150=300 (100.0)** |

Source: Field Study

As per the table delay in sanctioning loan is the most important problem in taking loans from institutional agencies in the opinion of 101 (33.7) respondents. Farmers need timely delivery of credit to carry on agricultural operations. Credit delivery from the institutional agencies is not prompt and adequate. The second major problem is difficulty in documentation. Institutional agencies ask for a number of papers. Rural people, mostly weaker sections cannot submit them. Some from households possess assigned lands. They have difficulty in establishing ownership. 92 (30.6) respondents hold this opinion. 77 (25.6) respondents state that "Unfavorable terms of repayment" is a problem. Institutions demand timely repayment. They do not mind the problems of the borrowers. Dependency on the middle men is another problem. Rural people cannot negotiate directly with the institutional agencies. They have to depend on middle men. This problem is given by 30 (10.0) respondents. Respondents from all castes are of the same opinion. However, difficulty in documentation is given by more respondents in Khammam district in contrast to delay in sanctioning loans given by the respondents from Warangal district.

Some farm households in the rural areas take grain loans. The condition is that the borrowers should sell the crop to the lenders at the prevailing market price during harvest. Interest on such loans is very high. Repayment is on the spot when the crop is ready. 163 respondents in the study area have taken such loans. The following table shows the reason for grain loans.

**Table-3.2. Reasons for grain loans by the respondents**

| Caste | Purpose | | |
|---|---|---|---|
| | Agricultural inputs | Domestic purpose | Others |
| BC | 7+18=25<br>(23.3) | 2+4=6<br>(14.6) | 0+0=0<br>(0.0) |
| SC | 15+16=31<br>(28.1) | 5+10=15<br>(36.5) | 3+3=6<br>(40.0) |
| ST | 18+33=51<br>(47.6) | 8+12=20<br>(48.7) | 4+5=9<br>(60.0) |
| Total | 40+67=107<br>(65.6) | 15+26=41<br>(25.1) | 7+8=15<br>(9.2) |

Source: Field Study

107 (65.6) respondents have taken grain loans to purchase agricultural inputs. Farmers need credit on the spot to purchase seeds, fertilizers and pesticides. They cannot weight for loans as agricultural operations are timely. 41 (25.1) respondents have taken grain loans for domestic purposes. Ill health, child education, child birth, death of the family members and the like force the rural people to borrow on the spot. Other reasons are given by 15 (9.2) respondents which are of contingent in nature. BC and ST respondents are small in number to take such loans when compared to ST respondents. Around 92 per cent of the ST respondents have taken grain loans accepting the terms of the lenders. These loans are small amounts carrying high rate of

interest. Respondents in Khammam district are more (108) in taking such loans than the respondents in Warangal district.

Utilisation of loan for the purpose is examined in the following table.

**Table-3.3. Number of respondents not using the loans for the purpose**

| Caste | Used for the purpose | Diverted for other purposes | Total |
|---|---|---|---|
| BC | 24+23=47 (39.1) | 31+23=54 (30.0) | 55+46=101 (33.7) |
| SC | 21+19=40 (33.3) | 36+36=72 (40.0) | 57+55=112 (37.3) |
| ST | 18+15=33 (27.5) | 20+34=54 (30.0) | 38+49=87 (29.0) |
| Total | 63+57=120 (40.0) | 87+93=180 (60.0) | 150+150=300 (100.0) |

Source: Field Study

Farmers take loans keeping a purpose in their mind but when it comes to utilisation there is the problem of diversion. Uncontrollable situations force the farmers to divert the borrowed amounts. 180 (60.0) respondents have diverted the loans for other purposes. It implies that only 120 (40.0) respondents spend the loan for the purpose. Normally, loans are taken for productive activities. But utilisation may be for unproductive activities. Diversation disturb the household plans for higher incomes. Along with interest they go on increasing. Some rural families are helpless in checking the problem of diversations. Diversations are more among the SC and ST respondents. They are more among the respondents of Khammam district than in Warangal district.

Areas to which credit is diverted are analysed in the following table.

**Table-3.4. Expenditure areas to which credit is diverted**

| Caste | Family functi ons | Consump tion needs | Health problem s | Children Educatio n | Two or more | Total |
|---|---|---|---|---|---|---|
| BC | 4+3 =7 (31.8) | 6+5 =11 (39.2) | 8+9 =17 (30.3) | 9+3 =12 (38.7) | 4+3 =7 (16.2) | 31+23 =54 (30.0) |
| SC | 6+4 =10 (45.4) | 4+7 =11 (39.2) | 10+12 =22 (39.2) | 7+5 =12 (38.7) | 9+8 =17 (39.5) | 36+36 =72 (40.0 |
| ST | 1+4 =5 (22.7) | 2+4 =6 (21.4) | 4+13 =17 (30.3) | 3+4 =7 (22.5) | 10+9 =19 (44.1) | 20+34 =54 (9.0) |
| Total | 11+11 =22 (12.2) | 12+16 · =28 (15.5) | 22+34 =56 (31.1) | 19+12 =31 (17.2) | 23+20 =43 (23.8) | 87+93 =180 (100.0) |

Source: Field Study

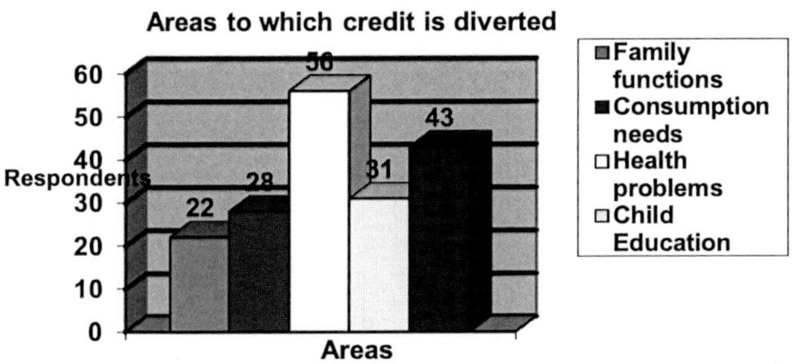


As per the above table 180 respondents have diverted credit for purposes other than for which it was borrowed. Out of 300 respondents diversion is by 60 per cent of the respondents. Diversion of credit is mostly to spend on health problems as shown in the above table. 56 (31.1) respondents have diverted for this purpose. The next area to which diversion has taken place is children education, 31 (17.2) respondents have diverted for this purpose. 28 (15.5) respondents have diverted to consumption needs followed by 22 (12.2) respondents to family functions. 43 (23.8) respondents have diverted the loans taken to different purposes and so the diversion is a mix up by them. Family functions, health problems and children education are important areas of diversion by SC respondents. Health problems, children education and consumption needs are important areas of diversion to BC respondents. Health problems, children education are important to ST respondents. Diversion is by more respondents (93) in Khammam district when compared to the respondent (87) in Warangal districts.

Reasons for the increase in the overall debt of the respondents year to year are analysed in the following table.

**Table-3.5. Reasons for increase in the overall debt year to year of the respondents**

| Caste | Reasons | | | | | | | |
|---|---|---|---|---|---|---|---|---|
| | **Crop failure** | **Limited employment opportunities** | **Increasing cost of child education** | **Mounting medical cost** | **Growing cost of living** | **Increasing cost of cultivation** | **Two or more** | **Total** |
| BC | 1+1 =2 (18.1) | 5+4 =9 (29.0) | 13+8 =21 (43.7) | 3+4 =7 (18.9) | 13+4 =17 (42.5) | 2+9= 11 (27.5) | 18+16 =34 (36.5) | 55+46 =101 (33.7) |
| SC | 1+3 =4 (36.3) | 5+6 =11 (35.4) | 9+6 =15 (31.2) | 8+5 =13 (35.1) | 10+3 =13 (32.5) | 2+14 =16 (56.0) | 22+18 =40 (43.0) | 57+55 =112 (37.3) |
| ST | 3+2 =5 (45.4) | 7+4 =11 (35.4) | 7+5 =12 (25.0) | 9+8 =17 (45.9) | 8+2 =10 (25.0) | 1+12 =13 (32.5) | 3+16 =19 (20.4) | 38+49 =87 (29.0) |
| **Total** | **5+6 =11 (3.6)** | **17+14 =31 (10.3)** | **29+19 =48 (16.0)** | **20+17 =37 (12.3)** | **31+9 =40 (13.3)** | **5+35 =40 (13.3)** | **43+50 =93 (31.0)** | **150+150 =300 (100.0)** |

Source: Field Study

To sum up increasing cost of child education, increasing cost of living and cultivation and expenditure on health care are the major reasons for the growing indebtedness in rural India. Increasing cost of cultivation is given by more respondents from Khammam district where as increasing cost of child education is given by more respondents from Warangal district as the reason.

Indian farmers are deeply attached to land ownership. Land ownership adds to the prestige of the family in their opinion. They are inclined to purchase additional land by borrowing. Sale or purchase of land by the respondents is examined in the following table.

**Table-3.6. Purchase or sale of land by the respondents**

| Caste | Purchase of land | Sale of land | Both | Total |
|---|---|---|---|---|
| BC | 11+7=18 (56.2) | 2+0=2 (11.1) | 8+13=21 (38.1) | 21+20=41 (39.0) |
| SC | 6+3=9 (28.1) | 5+4=9 (50.0) | 6+10=16 (29.0) | 17+17=34 (32.3) |
| ST | 4+1=5 (15.6) | 3+4=7 (38.8) | 4+14=18 (32.7) | 11+19=30 (28.5) |
| Total | 21+11=32 (30.4) | 10+8=18 (17.1) | 18+37=55 (52.3) | 49+56=105 (100.0) |

Source: Field Study

32 (30.4) respondents have purchased land. 18 BC respondents, 09 SC respondents and 05 ST respondents are among the purchaser. 18 (17.1) respondents have sold out of land. Sale of land is more by SC respondents (9), ST respondents (7) and BC respondents only (2). It is clearly that BC respondents purchase land and do not prefer to sell out. 55 (52.3) respondents are both sellers and purchasers. Here also BC respondents are more in number (21) followed by ST (18) and SC (16) respondents. 105 respondents in total area involved in

the process of sale and purchase of land. Respondents from Warangal are more in number sale-purchase process.

Normally farmers do not sell land. It is not only affixed asset but also a means of livelihood. More over sale of land under mines the family status in the rural societies. Under inevitable conditions and also to acquired new assets farmers may sell land. 73 respondents in the study area have sold land. Reasons for the sale of land by the respondents are examined as follows.

**Table-3.7. Reasons for the sale of land by the respondents**

| Caste | Reasons | | | | | | | Total |
|---|---|---|---|---|---|---|---|---|
| | **Marriage** | **Festivals & Functions** | **To Clear old debts** | **Children Education** | **Health problem** | **More than one** | **House construction & House hold assets** | |
| BC | 3+1 =4 (40.0) | 1+2 =3 (50.0) | 5+3 =8 (30.7) | 1+1 =2 (16.6) | 2+1= 3 (42.8) | 1+1= 2 (28.5) | 0+1 =1 (20.0) | 13+10 =23 (31.5) |
| SC | 2+1 =3 (30.0) | 1+1 =2 (33.3) | 7+4 =11 (42.3) | 2+2 =4 (33.3) | 1+1= 2 (28.5) | 3+1= 4 (57.1) | 2+2 =4 (80.0) | 18+12 =30 (41.0) |
| ST | 2+1 =3 (30.0) | 1+0 =1 (16.7) | 4+3 =7 (26.9) | 3+3 =6 (50.0) | 1+1= 2 (28.5) | 0+1= 1 (14.2) | 0+0 =0 (0.0) | 11+9 =20 (27.3) |
| **Total** | **7+3 =10 (13.6)** | **3+3 =6 (8.2)** | **16+10 =26 (35.6)** | **6+6 =12 (16.4)** | **4+3 =7 (9.5)** | **4+3 =7 (9.5)** | **2+3 =5 (6.8)** | **42+31 =73 (100.0)** |

Source: Field Study

As per the above table the most important reason for the sale of land is the need to clear of old debts. 26 (35.6) respondents have sold land for this reason only. Children education has become costly in the light of privatisation. 12 (16.4) respondents have sold land to meet the expenditure on education. Performance of marriages has become a costly affair and 10 (13.6) respondents have sold for this reason. Festivals and functions are to be celebrated and for this purpose 6 (8.2) respondents have sold land. 7 (9.5) respondents have sold land for health care expenditure and 05 respondents for house construction and to acquire house hold assets like T.V, Byke etc. 7 (9.5) respondents state more than one reason for the sale of land. SCs are more in number to sell land followed by BCs and STs. Even ST respondents with in their tradition and culture have sold land for marriage performance. Sale of land for house construction is given has reason by 04 SC respondents and just 01 and 0 by BC and ST respondents. Respondents in Warangal district (42) are more in selling out land when compared to 31 respondents in Khammam district.

Purchase of land and sale of land are a regular feature in the Indian villages. Purchase implies sales and vice versa. Some respondents have both sold and purchased land. The following table gives the sources of finance for purchasing land.

**Table-3.8. Source of finance for purchase of land**

| Caste | Agricultural income saved | Institutional loans | Non-Institutional loans | Sale of assets | Two or more sources | Total |
|---|---|---|---|---|---|---|
| BC | 7+7 =14 (43.7) | 3+3 =6 (60.0) | 2+4 =6 (28.5) | 3+2 =5 (62.5) | 5+3 =8 (50.0) | 20+19 =39 (44.8) |
| SC | 6+5 =11 (34.3) | 2+1 =3 (30.0) | 3+4 =7 (33.3) | 0+1 =1 (12.5) | 2+1 =3 (18.7) | 13+12 =25 (28.7) |
| ST | 4+3 =7 (21.8) | 1+0=1 (10.0) | 5+3 =8 (38.0) | 1+1 =2 (25.0) | 3+2 =5 (31.2) | 14+9 =23 (26.4) |
| **Total** | **17+15 =32 (36.7)** | **6+4 =10 (11.4)** | **10+11 =21 (24.1)** | **4+4 =8 (9.1)** | **10+6 =16 (18.3)** | **47+40 =87 (100.0)** |

Source: Field Study

87 respondents have purchased land in the study area. 32 (36.7) respondents have save from agricultural incomes and purchased the land. 21 (24.1) respondents have taken loans from non-institutional sources to buy land. 8 (9.1) respondents have sold out assets while 10 (11.4) respondents have borrowed from institutional sources. 16 (18.3) respondents have availed two or more sources. BC respondents are more in saving agricultural incomes and also in raising institutional loans. They are at top (39) respondents followed by SC (25) and ST (23) respondents. Non-institutional loans are more for purchasing land by the ST respondents. BC respondents are more in utilising two or more sources followed by ST and SC respondents. Respondents (47) in Warangal are more in purchasing land than the respondents (40) in Khammam district. Agricultural income as a source to purchase land is also more in Warangal district.

Non-institutional agencies use force and threats to recover credit dues along with interest. The rate of interest, they charge, is irrational. Interest rate depend on the needs of the borrowers and repaying capacity. In the name of loan and exorbitant rates of interest they grab the land of the borrowers. The week and humble sections of the rural society remain as spectators and surrender rights on landed property. The following table gives the details of land occupation by the non-institutional agencies.

**Table-3.9. Occupied land of the respondents by the non-institutional agencies**

| Caste | Occupied | Extent of land (in acres) |
|---|---|---|
| BC | 2+5=7 (21.8) | 1.0+10.0=11.0 |
| SC | 4+6=10 (31.2) | 6.0+18.0=24.0 |
| ST | 7+8=15 (46.8) | 11.0+25.0=36.0 |
| **Total** | **13+19=32 (100.0)** | **18.0+53.0=71.0** |

Source: Field Study

Occupation problem is more to ST respondents (15) followed by SC respondents (10) and BC respondents only (7). Extent of land occupied is also more with regard to ST (36 acres) and SC (24 acres) respondents. Only 11 acres of the land of the BC respondents is under occupation by the non-institutional agencies.

Allotment of land to the respondents under land reforms is given in the following table.

**Table-3.10. Allotment of land to the respondents under land reforms**

| Caste | **Allotted** | **Extent of Land (in acres)** | **Not allotted** | **Total** |
|---|---|---|---|---|
| BC | 5+2=7 (10.1) | 8.0+3.0= 11.0 | 50+44=94 (40.6) | 55+46=101 (33.7) |
| SC | 13+8=21 (30.4) | 19.0+18.0= 37.0 | 44+47=91 (39.3) | 57+55=112 (37.3) |
| ST | 19+22=41 (59.4) | 28.0+63.0= 91.0 | 19+27=46 (19.9) | 38+49=87 (29.0) |
| **Total** | **37+32=69 (100.0)** | **55.0+84.0 =139.0** | **113+118=231 (100.0)** | **150+150=300 (100.0)** |

Source: Field Study

69 respondents, as given in the above table are the beneficiaries under land reforms. 37 are from Warangal and 32 are from Khammam districts. ST respondents are (41) the minimum beneficiaries. 21 SC respondents and only 07 BC respondents are also benefited. 139 acres of land is allotted to 69 respondents in the study area. Here also STs are the maximum beneficiaries with 91 acres of land. SC respondents have received 37 acres and BC respondents only 11acres. Land reforms, in the study area, have benefited ST and SC respondents. In terms of respondents Warangal district is benefited more where as in terms of area Khammam respondents are benefited to the maximum. The data in the

above table indicates that 23 percent of the respondents are the beneficiaries from land reforms.

Central and State government have conceived different programs to help the farmers in the rural society, more so the weaker sections of the farming community. Beneficiaries of the government programs are shown in the following table.

**Table-3.11. Beneficiaries of the Government programs**

| Caste | Loan Mora-torium | Incen-tives | Subsidised rate of interest | No benefit | Total |
|---|---|---|---|---|---|
| BC | 29+13 =42 (32.5) | 9+8 =17 (48.5) | 10+2 =12 (16.2) | 7+5 =12 (24.0) | 55+46 =101 (33.7) |
| SC | 26+21 =47 (36.4) | 7+4 =11 (31.4) | 13+17 =30 (40.5) | 11+10 =21 (42.0) | 57+55 =112 (37.3) |
| ST | 21+19 =40 (31.0) | 4+3 =7 (20.0) | 7+14 =21 (28.3) | 6+11 =17 (34.0) | 38+49 =87 (29.0) |
| **Total** | **76+53 =129 (43.0)** | **20+15 =35 (11.6)** | **30+44 =74 (24.6)** | **24+26 =50 (16.6)** | **150+150 =300 (100.0)** |

Source: Field Study

Only50 respondents are not benefited in any form as given in the above table. It implies that more than 83 percent are benefited in some form or other. 129 (43.0) respondents have enjoyed loan moratorium. 35 respondents have received incentives from the government. Subsidised rate of interest is available to 74 (24.6) respondents. SCs are more in numbers with regard to incentives whereas SC respondents followed by ST respondents are more to receive subsidised rate of interest. SCs are more to benefit from land moratorium programms also. Respondents from Warangal district are more in number to get the benefits from moratorium and incentives. Respondents from

Khammam are more in number to available to benefit of subsidised rate of interest.

Indebtedness affects the overall existence of the individual. He loses self-confidence and always in tension, inferiority complexes develop, especially, in rural society. Implications of rural indebtedness are analysed from different angles and the following table examines the status of the respondents before the lenders in the society. Status is estimated by using scaling method.

## Implications

**Table-3.12. Status of the respondents in view of the indebtedness**

| Caste | Before the lender | | | In the society | | | Total |
|---|---|---|---|---|---|---|---|
| | Very low | Low | Normal | Very low | Low | Normal | |
| BC | 4+3 =7 (17.9) | 9+7 =16 (24.2) | 42+36 =78 (40.0) | 5+8 =13 (38.2) | 11+12 =23 (24.4) | 39+26 =65 (37.7 | 55+46 =101 (33.7) |
| SC | 7+8 =15 (38.4) | 13+15 =28 (42.4) | 37+32 =69 (35.3) | 4+6 =10 (29.4) | 15+18 =33 (35.1) | 38+31 =69 (40.1) | 57+55 =112 (37.3) |
| ST | 8+9 =17 (43.5) | 10+12 =22 (33.3) | 20+28 =48 (24.6) | 6+5 =11 (32.3) | 17+21 =38 (40.4) | 15+23 =38 (22.0) | 38+49 =87 (29.0) |
| **Total** | **19+20 =39 (13.0)** | **32+34 =66 (22.0)** | **99+96 =195 (65.0)** | **15+19 =34 (11.3)** | **43+51 =94 (31.3)** | **92+80 =172 (57.3)** | **150+150 =300 (100.0)** |
| 150 (100.0) | | | | 150 (100.0) | | | |

Source: Field Study

In the above table status of the respondents before the lenders and in the society are examined. It is happy to note that 195 (65.0) respondents state that their status before the lender is normal. However 66 (22.0) respondents feel that their status low before the lender. 39 (13.0) respondents to state that their status is very low. In other words low status. before the lender is evident among 105 (35.0) respondents. BCs in view of their upcoming efforts are limited in the low status category. SC and ST respondents suffer more from the low status before the lender.

Status in the society is also analysed in the above table. Rural societies are more interested in spreading personal and family problems. Any in convenience or incident in a house hold becomes a matter for public discussion. Indebtedness, after some times, becomes open for public discussion. Status of the indebted house hold gets disturbed over the period. 172 (57.3) respondents state that their status is normal. It implies that the status of 128 (42.6) respondents is below normal or low. 13 (38.2) respondents status that their status is very low due to indebtedness. Whereas 94 (31.3) respondents state that their status is low. BCs are comfortable to some extent in the society when compared to SCs and STs. The status of STs is less in the normal category. More respondents in Warangal district maintain normal status before the lenders and in the society when compared to the respondents of Khammam district.

Relations of the respondents with the lenders and the people in the locality are examined. Growing indebtedness makes the individual easily irritable. Relations with the people around may get strained. This aspect of the implications of indebtedness is examined in the following table.

**Table-3.13. Relations of the respondents with the lenders and the people in the society**

| Caste | With the lenders | | | With the locals | | | Total |
|---|---|---|---|---|---|---|---|
| | Very smooth | Smooth | Quarrels / Some | Very smooth | Smooth | Quarrels / Some | |
| BC | 8+6 =14 (56.0) | 14+11 =25 (32.4) | 33+29 =62 (31.3) | 6+5 =11 (47.8) | 12+10 =22 (32.8 | 37+31 =68 (32.3) | 55+46 =101 (33.7) |

| | | | | | | | |
|---|---|---|---|---|---|---|---|
| SC | 5+3=8 (32.0) | 16+13 =29 (37.6) | 36+39 =75 (37.8) | 4+3 =7 (30.4) | 14+12 =26 (38.8) | 39+40 =79 (37.6) | 57+55 =112 (37.3) |
| ST | 2+1 =3 (12.0) | 10+13 =23 (29.3) | 26+35 =61 (30.8) | 3+2 =5 (21.7) | 9+10 =19 (28.3) | 26+37 =63 (30.0) | 38+49 =87 (29.0) |
| **Total** | **15+10= 25 (8.3)** | **40+37 =77 (25.6)** | **95+103 =198 (66.0)** | **13+10= 23 (7.6)** | **35+32 =67 (22.3)** | **102+108 =210 (70.0)** | **150+15 0=300 (100.0)** |
| 150 (100.0) | | | | 150 (100.0) | | | |

Source: Field Study

198 (66.0) respondents as given in the above table are quarrelsome with the lender. There are arguments and counter arguments on small issues also. 77 (25.6) respondents state that their relations with the lenders are smooth. 25 (8.3) respondents mention that their relations with the lenders are very smooth. More respondents in Khammam district exhibit quarrels some nature when compared to the respondents of Waranga; district.

Guilty feeling and inferiority affect the relations of the indebted people with the locals. They feel that everyone in the locality thinks about them and their debt. 210 (70.0) respondents in the study area have no smooth relations with the people in the locality. On petty issues there are quarrels and arguments. 67 (22.3) respondents maintain smooth relations while 23 (7.6) respondents have very smooth relations. It implies that 30 percent of the respondents maintain good relations with the people of the area. Here also respondents in Warangal are comparatively better.

Money lenders and private agencies use force and threats to recover credit dues and sometimes to usurp land and other property. This angle of the implications is examined in the following table.

**Table-3.14. Threats to the respondents from money lenders**

| Caste | Often | Sometimes | Rarely | Never | Total |
|---|---|---|---|---|---|
| BC | 2+0 =2 (5.8) | 1+5 =6 (16.6) | 8+10 =18 (39.1) | 44+31 =75 (40.5) | 55+46 =101 (33.7) |
| SC | 5+9 =14 (41.1) | 4+12 =16 (44.4) | 13+8 =21 (45.6) | 35+27 =62 (33.5) | 57+55 =112 (37.3) |
| ST | 7+11 =18 (52.9) | 5+9 =14 (38.8) | 7+0 =7 (15.2) | 19+29 =48 (25.9) | 38+49 =87 (29.0) |
| **Total** | **14+20 =34 (11.3)** | **10+26 =36 (12.0)** | **28+18 =46 (15.3)** | **98+87 =185 (61.6)** | **150+150 =300 (100.0)** |

Source: Field Study

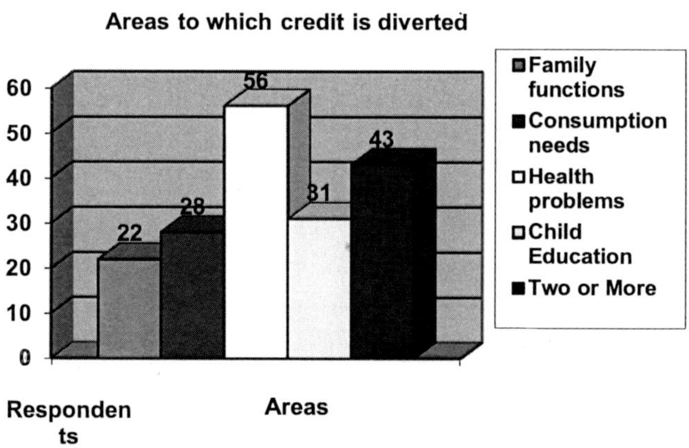


As per the above table 185 (61.6) respondents state that such problems of threat have never taken place. It implies that there are threats to the remaining 38.4 percent of the respondents. Threats are often in the opinion of 34 (11.3) respondents. 36 (12.0) respondents state that there are threats some times, not often. Threats are rare as given by 46 (15.3) respondents. Threats and intimidation are comparatively more in

Khammam district than in Warangal district. BC respondents are comfortable as only 26 of them face threats of different degrees.

Growing indebtedness of individual disturbs the relations with the family members. They lose balance and patience and the result is strained relations with the family members. This aspect of implications is examined in the following table.

**Table-3.15. Relations of the respondents with family members in the wake of indebtedness**

| Caste | Very cordial | Cordial | Not cordial | Disturbing | Total |
|---|---|---|---|---|---|
| BC | 13+12 =25 (47.1) | 14+10 =24 (30.7) | 8+13 =21 (31.3) | 20+11 =31 (30.3) | 55+46 =101 (33.7) |
| SC | 8+9 =17 (32.0) | 12+12 =24 (30.7) | 16+14 =30 (44.7) | 21+20 =41 (40.1) | 57+55 =112 (37.3) |
| ST | 5+6 =11 (20.7) | 15+15 =30 (38.4) | 10+6 =16 (23.8) | 8+22 =30(29.4) | 38+49 =87 (29.0) |
| Total | 26+27 =53 (17.6) | 41+37 =78 (26.0) | 34+33 =67 (22.3) | 49+53 =102 (34.0) | 150+150 =300 (100.0) |

Source: Field Study

Disturbing relations are more among the SC respondents followed by BC and ST respondents. Not cordial relations are also among ST respondents in the study area. Both the districts of study area close in numbers with regard to the relations with the family members.

Closely related to the aspect analysed in the previous table is at home behavior of the respondents due to indebtedness. The following table gives the behavior pattern of the respondents at home.

**Table-3.16. At home behaviour of the respondents due to indebtedness**

| Caste | Always quarrels | Occasional quarrels | No quarrels | Total |
|---|---|---|---|---|
| BC | 4+6 =10 (15.8) | 19+16 =35 (35.3) | 32+24 =56 (40.5) | 55+46 =101 (33.7) |
| SC | 14+13 =27 (42.8) | 16+20 =36 (36.3) | 27+22 =49 ( 35.5) | 57+55 =112 (37.3) |
| ST | 11+15 =26 (41.2) | 13+15 =28 (28.2) | 14+19 =33 (23.9) | 38+49 =87 (29.0) |
| Total | 29+34 =63 (21.0) | 48+51 =99 (33.0) | 73+65 =138 (46.0) | 150+150 =300 (100.0) |

Source: Field Study

138 (46.0) respondents state that they have no quarrels at home due to indebtedness. 63 (21.0) respondents say that they always quarrels on small issues at home by losing temper. 99 (33.0) respondents state that there are quarrels occasionally. It implies that 54.0 percent of the respondents quarrel at home with family members. BCs are at the top to maintain peaceful homes without quarrels followed by SCs and STs. In the always quarreling category STs come first followed by SCs and BCs. More respondents from Warangal conduct them self at home without quarrels.

It is quite natural for people to share their problems with others and in such interactions, solutions and suggestions come out. Sharing of the problem with others relieves the burden to some extent and confidence starts to grow. The sharing of the feelings on indebtedness by the respondents is examined here under.

**Table-3.17. Sharing of feelings by the respondents on problem with**

| Caste | Friends | Elders in the social group | Parents | Close relatives | Wife & children | More than one | Not sharing | Total |
|---|---|---|---|---|---|---|---|---|
| BC | 7+5=12 (50.0) | 1+3=4 (22.2) | 3+1=4 (20.0) | 0+4=4 (23.5) | 14+7=21 (33.3) | 21+18=39 (34.5) | 9+8=17 (35.4) | 55+46=101 (33.7) |
| SC | 4+2=6 (25.0) | 2+4=6 (33.3) | 5+2=7 (35.0) | 5+1=6 (35.2) | 11+11=22 (34.9) | 19+21=40 (35.3) | 11+14=25 (58.1) | 57+55=112 (37.3) |
| ST | 5+1=6 (25.0) | 2+6=8 (50.0) | 4+5=9 (45.0) | 5+2=7 (41.1) | 7+13=20 (31.7) | 15+16=31 (30.0) | 0+6=6 (2.3) | 38+49=87 (29.0) |
| **Total** | **16+8=24 (8.0)** | **5+13=18 (6.0)** | **12+8=20 (6.6)** | **10+7=17 (5.6)** | **32+31=63 (21.0)** | **55+55=110 (36.6)** | **20+28=48 (16.0)** | **150+150=300 (100.0)** |

Source: Field Study

As per the above table 48 (16.0) respondents do not share their problem of debt burden with anyone. SCs are more in this category followed by BCs and SCs. 252 (84.0) respondents share their feelings with friends, elders in the locality, parents, close relatives and wife and children. 110 (6.6) respondents share their problem with more than one agency. 63 (21.0) respondents share their problem with wife and children. 24 (8.0) respondents share with friends, 20 with parents, 18 with elders and 17 respondents open up with close relatives on the problem. All the three castes are identical to a great extent in sharing with wife and children. Parents are more important source of sharing by ST respondents. Friends are more important to BC respondents and elders are also more in importance as a source of sharing to STs. Non-sharing respondents are more in Khammam district. Sharing of the problem gives solace and helps to find a way out.

252 have stated in the previous table that they share their problems with different sources. There may be variations in the suggestions offered while sharing. Nature of the suggestions given to the respondents is analysed in the following table.

**Table-3.18. Nature of the suggestions given to the respondents while sharing**

| Caste | Very valuable | Valuable | Some what valuable | Not valuable | Total |
|---|---|---|---|---|---|
| BC | 7+4 =11 (25.0) | 11+14 =25 (37.8) | 7+8 =15 (45.4) | 21+12 =33 (28.9) | 46+38 =84 (33.3) |
| SC | 8+8 =16 (36.3) | 9+12 =21 (31.8) | 4+6 =10 (30.3) | 25+15 =40 (35.0) | 46+41 =87 (34.5) |
| ST | 8+9 =17 (38.6) | 9+11 =20 (30.3) | 3+5 =8 (24.2) | 23+18 =41 (35.9) | 38+43 =81 (32.1) |
| Total | 23+21 =44 (17.4) | 29+37 =66 (26.1) | 14+19 =33 (13.0) | 69+45 =114 (45.2) | 130+122 =252 (100.0) |

Source: Field Study

114 (45.2) respondents state that the suggestions floated during sharing are not valuable. 44 (17.4) respondents feel that the suggestions are very valuable. It is accepted by 66 (26.1) respondents that the suggestions offered are valuable. Together 43.5 percent of the respondents agree that the suggestions are valuable and useful. However 33 (13.0) respondents state that the suggestions are somewhat valuable. By and large more BC respondents accept that the suggestions are valuable in different degrees. 69 respondents are from Warangal stating that the suggestions are not valuable against 45 respondents stating so in Khammam district. Growing indebtedness, constraints the borrowers to seek help financially from near and dear. Necessity drives then to approach, friends, close relatives and social groups. This aspect of implications is analysed in the following table.

**Table-3.19. Financial assistance from close relatives, friends and social groups**

| Caste | Close relatives | | Friends | | Social groups | | Total |
|---|---|---|---|---|---|---|---|
| | Yes | No | Yes | No | Yes | No | |
| BC | 12+11 =23 (32.3) | 6+7 =13 (27.0) | 5+5 =10 (32.2) | 3+12 =15 (36.5) | 17+8 =25 (35.2) | 12+3 =15 (39.4) | 55+46 =101 (33.7) |
| SC | 11+15 =26 (36.6) | 5+9 =14 (29.1) | 7+3 =10 (32.2) | 1+10 =11 (26.8) | 19+14 =33 (46.4) | 14+4 =18 (47.3) | 57+55 =112 (37.3) |
| ST | 9+13 =22 (30.9) | 6+15 =21 (43.7) | 7+4 =11 (35.4) | 9+6 =15 (36.5) | 5+8 =13 (18.3) | 2+3 =5 (13.1) | 38+49 =87 (29.0) |
| Total | 32+39 =71 (23.6) | 17+31 =48 (16.0) | 19+12 =31 (10.3) | 13+28 =41 (13.6) | 41+30 =71 (23.6) | 28+10 =38 (12.6) | 150+150=300 (100.0) |

Source: Field Study

As per the above table 71 (23.6) respondents seek financial assistance from close relations. Respondents in Khammam are more to get help from close relatives. 31 (10.3) respondents take financial help from friends. ST respondents are more in this category. 71 (23.6) respondents take financial assistance from social groups. SC respondents are more in this category followed by BC and ST respondents. In all 173 respondents have received financial support from the three important sources. It implies that 127 respondents in the study area have not received any financial assistance from friends, close relatives and social groups. They have to struggle on their own to meet their financial needs. Social groups and friends are more important in extending help to the respondents in Warangal district whereas close relatives are important in Khammam district.

Threats, use of force seizing of property, constant reminders are some of the practices of the microfinance institutions. Their role credit delivery is being questioned and recently the RBI has issued guidelines to the MFIs for compliance. Rural people are illiterate and ignorant and financially week. They suffer from the practices of the microfinance institutions to a large extent. To assess the awareness of respondents on the practices of the MFIs data is processed in the following table.

**Table-3.20. Awareness of the respondents about the micro credit structure and practices**

| Caste | Complete | Some extent | Little extent | No | Total |
|---|---|---|---|---|---|
| BC | 12+13<br>=25<br>(25.5) | 6+4<br>=10<br>(16.9) | 2+2<br>=4<br>(17.3) | 35+27<br>=62<br>(51.6) | 55+46<br>=101<br>(33.7) |
| SC | 21+18<br>=39<br>(39.7) | 14+11<br>=25<br>(42.3) | 7+4<br>=11<br>(47.8) | 15+22<br>=37<br>(30.8) | 57+55<br>=112<br>(37.3) |

| ST | 18+16 =34 (34.6) | 12+12 =24 (40.6) | 3+5 =8 (34.7) | 5+16 =21 (17.5) | 38+49 =87 (29.0) |
|---|---|---|---|---|---|
| Total | 51+47 =98 (32.6) | 32+27 =59 (19.6) | 12+11 =23 (7.6) | 55+65 =120 (40.0) | 150+150 =300 (100.0) |

Source: Field Study

As per the above table 120 (40.0) respondents are not aware of the credit delivery and methods of repayment of the MFIs. More respondents from BC category have no idea followed by 37 from SC and 21 from ST categories. Complete awareness is stated by 98 (32.6) respondents. 59 (19.6) respondents have awareness to some extent and 23 (7.6) respondents are aware to a little extent. This ignorance of the rural areas is misused by the MFIs. Awareness is more in Warangal district when compared to Khammam district.

Growing indebtedness affects the health of the borrowers. Tension, frustration, helplessness and constant thinking create health problems to the respondents. The following table analyses the health problems of the respondents due to indebtedness.

**Table-3.21. Health problems of the respondents due to indebtedness**

| Caste | More | Little extent | Less | No problem | Total |
|---|---|---|---|---|---|
| BC | 10+11 =21 (28.7) | 5+4 =9 (25.0) | 11+15 =26 (25.2) | 29+16 =45 (51.1) | 55+46 =101 (33.7) |
| SC | 11+13 =24 (32.8) | 7+7 =14 (38.8) | 17+22 =39 (37.8) | 22+13 =35 (39.7) | 57+55 =112 (37.3) |
| ST | 13+15 =28 (38.3) | 7+6 =13 (36.1) | 14+24 =38 (36.8) | 4+4 =8 (9.0) | 38+49 =87 (29.0) |
| **Total** | **34+39 =73 (24.3)** | **19+17 =36 (12.0)** | **42+61 =103 (34.3)** | **55+33 =88 (29.3)** | **150+150 =300 (100.0)** |

Source: Field Study

88 (29.3) respondents have no health problems. This is a welcome feature. 103 (34.3) respondents have very few problems. 36 (12.0) respondents have problems to a little extent. 73 (24.3) respondents suffer from more health problems. 45 BC respondents have no health problems followed by 35 SC respondents and only 8 ST respondents. ST respondents are more in number with high incidence of health problems followed by SC and BC respondents. The health of BC and SC respondents is better than that of the ST respondents. Warangal district has more no problems respondents than Khammam district. In other words health problems are less among the respondents of Warangal district.

Health problems of the respondents are analysed in the above table 5.21. Growing indebtedness disturbs the borrowers and create health problems to themselves and family members. They cannot pay due attention to the overall health of the family members. Finance becomes a constraint in attending to health care of the family members. The following table analyses health care measures provided by the respondents to the family members.

**Table-3.22. Health care of the family members of the respondents**

| **Caste** | **Effective** | **Little effective** | **Not effective** | **Negligible** | **Total** |
|---|---|---|---|---|---|
| BC | 7+6 =13 (43.3) | 12+14 =26 (38.8) | 6+4 =10 (28.5) | 30+22 =52 (30.9) | 55+46 =101 (33.7) |
| SC | 4+9 =13 (43.3) | 12+10= 22 (32.8) | 5+8=13 (37.1) | 36+28 =64 (32.1) | 57+55 =112 (37.3) |
| ST | 3+1 =4 (13.3) | 8+11 =19 (28.3) | 7+5 =12 (34.2) | 20+32 =52 (30.9) | 38+49 =87 (29.0) |
| **Total** | **14+16=30 (10.0)** | **32+35 =67 (22.3)** | **18+17 =35 (11.7)** | **86+82 =168 (56.0)** | **150+150 =300 (100.0)** |

Source: Field Study

It is observed from the above table that only 30 (10.0) respondents have initiated effective health care measures. Health care measures are little effective as stated by 67 (23.3) respondents. Together less than 1/3rd of the respondents pay due attention to the health problems of the family members. 168 (56.0) respondents state that their health care measures are negligible.

It implies that they are unmindful and helpless in providing health care measures. 35 respondents initiate some measures which are not effective. These two categories together accounts for 67.7 per cent of the respondents in the study area. 2/3rd of the respondents are not careful to look after the health of the family members in view of their health problems of rural indebtedness. Khammam district is slightly better in providing health care to the family members then compared to Warangal district.

86 respondents from Warangal are in the "Negligible health care measures" against 82 respondents in Khammam district. The difference is marginal and most of the respondents in the study area are apathetic to initiate measures for promoting health of the family members.

Indebtedness acts like "Damocles's sword" on the borrowers. They are always in tension and their confidence levels are low. Future planning and hope for betterment in future are at low levels. They always think about repayment and plan for new loans by remaining in the debt trap. Some respondents may lose mental balance and frustration leading to depression. They lose interest in anything including agricultural activities. Incidence of depression among the respondents due to indebtedness is analysed in the following table.

**Table-3.23. Incidence of depression among the respondents due to indebtedness**

| Caste | More frequently | Frequently | Rarely | Never | Total |
|---|---|---|---|---|---|
| BC | 6+5 =11 | 8+6 =14 | 7+14 =21 | 34+21 =55 | 55+46 =101 |

| | | | | | |
|---|---|---|---|---|---|
| | (19.2) | (19.7) | (35.5) | (48.6) | (33.7) |
| SC | 10+13 =23 (40.3) | 15+12 =27 (38.0) | 11+12 =23 (38.9) | 21+18 =39 (34.5) | 57+55 =112 (37.3) |
| ST | 11+12=23 (40.3) | 16+14= 30 (42.2) | 8+7=1 5 (25.4) | 3+16=19 (16.8) | 38+49=8 7 (29.0) |
| **Total** | **27+30=57 (19.0)** | **39+32= 71 (23.6)** | **26+33 =59 (19.6)** | **58+55=113 (37.6)** | **150+150= 300 (100.0)** |

Source: Field Study

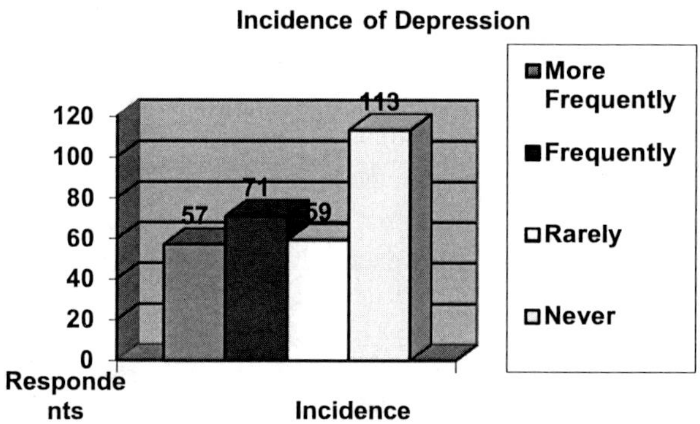


113 (37.6) respondents have never gone into depression. And this is a happy feature to note. However, 57 (19.0) respondents go into depression more frequently and 71 (23.6) respondents become depressed frequently. Joined together 42.6 per cent of the respondents suffer from depression. 59 (19.6) respondents rarely experience the problem of depression. Depression makes the individual passive and far from active pursuits. Problem of depression is more (20) to the respondents of Warangal district when compared to the respondents (62) of the Khammam district. Incidence is buy and large is identical in both the districts of the study. ST respondents and SC respondents are more prone to depression whereas BC respondents are a little comfortable. 55 BC respondents never have had this problem against 39 SC respondents and 19 ST respondents.

Frustration, irritation, helplessness, apathetic attitude to life, loss of interest in any work and pessimism may drive the individuals or family members to end life by restoring to suicides of late, in India suicide deaths by farmers are on the rise. Suicide attempts by the respondents or family members are examined in the following table.

**Table-3.24. Suicides attempt by the respondent family members**

| Caste | Yes | No | Total |
|---|---|---|---|
| BC | 13+15=28 (27.7) | 42+31=73 (36.6) | 55+46=101 (33.7) |
| SC | 15+18=33 (32.6) | 42+37=79 (39.6) | 57+55=112 (37.3) |
| ST | 19+21=40 (39.6) | 19+28=47 (23.6) | 38+49=87 (29.0) |
| Total | 47+54=101 (33.6) | 103+96=199(66.3) | 150+150=300 (100.0) |

Source: Field Study

It is observed from the above table that 101 (33.6) respondents have attempted to commit suicides. Suicide attempts are 39.6 among ST respondents followed by SC (32.6) and BC (27.7) respondents. BC respondents are less prone to suicide attempt as they are upcoming in rural areas. Attempts to commit suicides are more in Khammam district (54) than in Warangal district. 2/3rd of the respondents have not resorted to suicides and it is a happy feature in the study area.

When individual get vexed with their present occupation find it difficult to carry on as the future appears to be bleak they may shift to some other occupation depending on their eligibility with debt burden mounting up and dark shades over future some of the respondents may shift from agriculture in search of green pastures. This aspect of implications is analysed in the following table.

**Table-3.25. Opinion of the respondents to shift from present occupation**

| Caste | Yes | No | Total |
|---|---|---|---|
| BC | 16+18=34 (44.1) | 18+28=46 (20.6) | 55+46=101 (33.7) |
| SC | 12+12=24 (31.1) | 45+43=88 (39.4) | 57+55=112 (37.3) |
| ST | 9+10=19 (24.6) | 29+39=68 (30.4) | 38+49=87 (29.0) |
| Total | 37+40=77 (25.6) | 113+110=223 (74.3) | 150+150=300 (100.0) |

Source: Field Study

77 (25.6) respondents are positive to shift from cultivation. BC respondents (34) are more in accepting the proposition followed by SC (24) and ST (19) respondents. Occupational shift is opted by more respondents of Khammam district than of Warangal district. It is interesting to note that 223 (74.3) respondents are in no mood to change their occupation. Rural people have strong tie-ups with land and native village. They are not willing to leave the occupation and villages where their ancestors have lived for years together.

Urban centers provide job opportunities of a casual nature to the unskilled workers in sectors like construction, quarrying, domestic help and the like. Most of the rural people are devoid of skills. However, they feel that they can get work assignment of unskilled nature with regular income. They prefer migration to such centers in search of livelihood.

Such migrations from rural urban have been increasing during the last two decades of economic reforms. Migrations need not be permanent by the total family. Some physically fit members go, work, earn, save and send to their family to clear off debts. They maintain their contacts with the villages constantly. With a view to examine the desire to migrate data is processed in the following table.

**Table-3.26. Desire of the respondents to migrate to urban centers to increase income**

| Caste | Yes | No | Total |
|---|---|---|---|
| BC | 16+15=31 (40.2) | 39+31=70 (31.3) | 55+46=101 (33.7) |
| SC | 14+11=25 (32.4) | 43+44=87 (39.0) | 57+55=112 (37.3) |
| ST | 12+9=21 (27.2) | 26+40=66 (29.5) | 38+49=87 (29.0) |
| Total | 42+35=77 (25.6) | 108+115=223 (74.3) | 150+150=300 (100.0) |

Source: Field Study

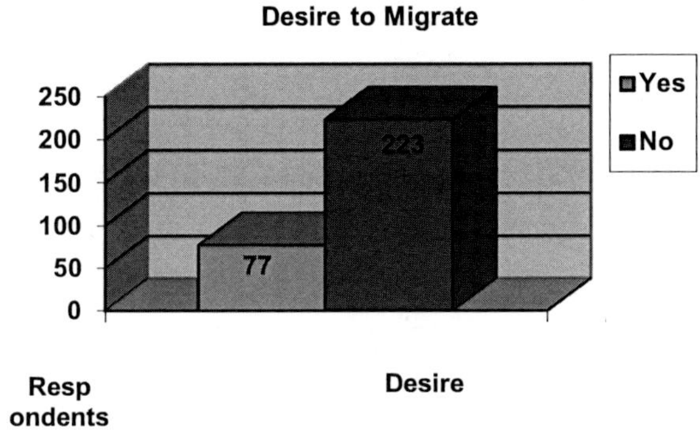


As per the above table only 77 respondents are willing to migrate 25.6 per cent of the respondents want to go to urban centres. It is a welcome trend as 75 per cent of the respondents, still, prefer to strive and struggle in the native villages. More BC respondents (40.2) followed by SC respondents (32.4) and ST respondents (27.2) are inclined to migrate with a desire to redeem debt by pooling up savings. More respondents (42) from Warangal district against (35) in Khammam are bent up on migration.

Cost of inputs has been increasing pushing up the cost of cultivation. Farmers of the weaker sections are not in a position to get proper remunerative prices for their produce. Of late, Crop Holiday has been declared in some areas as the value of the agricultural produce is not covering at least the cost. Farmers leave a part of cultivable land uncultivated.

Valuable natural resource, land, is kept idle even though it is cultivable. Farmers are afraid of additional borrowing to invest in cultivation as it would entail losses. This dimension of implications of Rural Indebtedness is explained in the following table.

**Table-3.27. Preference of the respondents to declare crop holiday**

| Caste | Yes | No | Total |
|---|---|---|---|
| BC | 0+18=18 (21.9 | 55+28=83 (38.0) | 55+46=101 (33.7) |
| SC | 5+20=25 (30.4) | 52+35=87 (39.9) | 57+55=112 (37.3) |
| ST | 16+23=39 (47.5) | 22+26=48 (22.0) | 38+49=87 (29.0) |
| Total | 21+61=82 (27.3) | 129+89=218 (72.6) | 150+150=300 (100.0) |

Source: Field Study

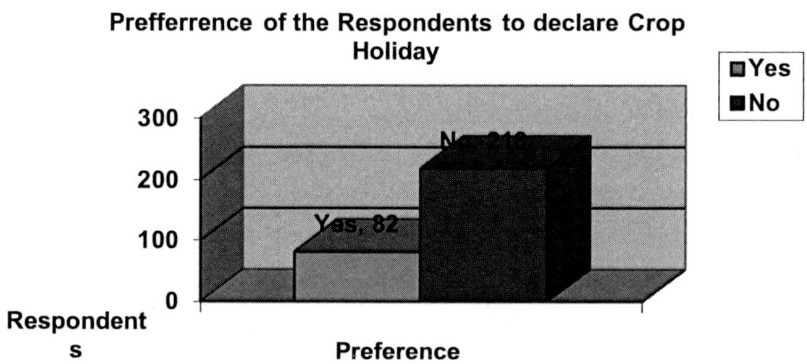


82 (27.3) respondents prefer Crop Holiday at least to save losses. They state that it is difficult to carry on cultivation. 39 (47.5) ST respondents followed by 25 (30.4) SC respondents and 18 (21.9) BC respondents prefer Crop Holiday to avoid costs with borrowings. However, only 21 respondents in Warangal district against 61 respondents in Khammam are prepared to declare Crop Holiday. No BC respondents prefers Crop Holiday in Warangal against 18 in Khammam district. Even in Khammam district BC respondents are less than ST and SC respondents to prefer Crop Holiday.

However, 72.6 per cent of the respondents in the study prefer to continue cultivation by accepting the odds in Cost-Revenue components. Indian farmer believes in land and agriculture continues, uninterrupted.

**Table-3.28. Planning by the respondents to overcome indebtedness**

| Caste | Controlling waste full expenditure | Generating more family income | Approach institutional sources | All | Not planning | Total |
|---|---|---|---|---|---|---|
| BC | 12+18 =30 (37.0) | 10+8 =18 (25.3) | 13+11 =24 (46.1) | 4+5 =9 (28.1) | 16+4 =20 (31.2) | 55+46 =101 (33.7) |
| SC | 14+15 =29 (35.8) | 15+17 =32 (45.0) | 11+7 =18 (34.6) | 3+8 =11 (34.7) | 14+8=22 (34.3) | 57+55 =112 (37.3) |
| ST | 10+12 =22 (27.1) | 11+10 =21 (29.5) | 5+5 =10 (19.2) | 2+10 =12 (37.5) | 10+12 =22 (34.3) | 38+49 =87 (29.0) |
| Total | 36+45 =81 (27.0) | 36+35 =71 (23.7) | 29+23 =52 (17.3) | 9+23 =32 (10.6) | 40+24 =64 (21.3) | 50+150 =300 (100.0) |

Source: Field Study

As per the above table 64 (21.3) respondents have no such plans. They leave the problem to time and are helpless. Respondents from all castes are near equal without any plans. 24 respondents from Khammam district against 40 respondents in Warangal district have no plans of redeeming debt burden. However, 81 respondents plan to control wasteful expenditure. This is a correct step in rural India as wasteful expenditure is unproductive and increases the overall debt burden. Khammam respondents are more in number to control wasteful expenditure than Warangal respondents. 30 BC respondents followed by 29 SC respondents and 22 ST respondents plan to control wasteful expenditure. So ST respondents need to tighten belts to reduce wasteful expenditure. 71 (23.7) respondents plan to generate more family income by taking up agro allied activities. This respondents in both district with this type of planning are near equal. 18 BC respondents 17 SC respondents and 10 ST respondents are under this type of planning. 52 (17.3) respondents plan to approach institutional sources for new loans to repay the non-institutional loans so as to reduce the burden of interest. Respondents from Warangal district are more 29 than Khammam respondents 23. BC respondents are more (24) followed by SC (18) respondents ST (10) respondents. 32 respondents want to adopt all the three plan types. Khammam respondents are more (23) against Warangal respondents only (9). ST (12) respondents are more in this combined plan by SC respondents (11) and BC respondents (9).

Policy measures have been introduced in India from time to time by the central and state Governments to combat the growing burden of rural indebtedness. The suggestions of the committees and commissions have been accepted and new channels of credit delivery, new institutions have all been created. But the problem persists eroding the very vitals of rural economy. The expectations of the respondents from the Government to reduce rural indebtedness are given in the following table.

**Table-3.29. Expectations of the respondents from the government to overcome the problems of indebtedness**

| Caste | Loan waiver | Low rate of interest | Subsidies on agricultural inputs | Remunerative prices &Crop insurance | Development of rural infrastructure | Control of inflation | More than one | Total |
|---|---|---|---|---|---|---|---|---|
| BC | 5+8 =13 (22.8) | 6+3 =9 (19.1) | 14+9 =23 (34.3) | 19+12 =31 (46.9) | 3+4 =7 (36.8) | 4+5 =9 (50.0) | 4+5 =9 (34.6) | 55+46 =101 (33.7) |
| SC | 12+13 =25 (43.8) | 8+10= 18 (38.2) | 10+11 =21 (31.3) | 18+8 =26 (39.3) | 2+6 =8 (42.1) | 2+3 =5 (27.7) | 5+4 =9 (34.6) | 57+55 =112 (37.3) |
| ST | 10+9 =19 (33.3) | 7+13= 20 (42.5) | 9+12 =21 (31.3) | 2+9 =11 (16.6) | 1+3 =4 (21.0) | 3+1 =4 (22.2) | 6+1 =7 (26.9) | 38+49 =87 (29.0) |
| **Total** | **27+30 =57 (19.0)** | **21+26= 47 (15.6)** | **35+32 =67 (22.3)** | **37+29 =66 (22.0)** | **6+13 =19 (6.3)** | **9+9 =18 (6.0)** | **15+11 =26 (8.6)** | **150+150=300 (100.0)** |

Source: Field Study

26 respondents opt for more than one implying the importance of all. There are variations in the expectations from

caste to caste. However, on basic suggestions the responses are close. Inter district expectations are also close to a considerable extent. Family needs and household requirement are many and they recur. 3 immediate requirements of the respondents are elicited and processed in the following table.

**Table-3.30. Three immediate requirements of the respondents**

| Requ-irements | BC | SC | ST | Total |
|---|---|---|---|---|
| Pucca house | 30+23 =53 (17.4) | 26+22 =48 (14.2) | 19+27 =46 (17.6) | 75+72 =147 (16.3) |
| Children Education | 42+34 =76 (25.0) | 40+27 =67 (19.9) | 17+18 =35 (13.4) | 99+79 =178 (19.7) |
| Children marriage | 27+21 =48 (15.8) | 48+42 =90 (26.7) | 26+25 =51 (19.5) | 101+88 =189 (21.0) |
| Medical care & treatment | 19+16 =35 (11.5) | 37+23 =60 (17.8) | 20+29 =49 (18.7) | 76+68 =144 (16.0) |
| Bore well | 8+7 =15 (4.9) | 7+8 =15 (4.4) | 11+16 =27 (10.3) | 26+31 =57 (6.3) |
| Diary activities | 9+8 =17 (5.6) | 6+7 =13 (3.8) | 8+9 =17 (6.5) | 23+24 =47 (5.2) |
| Household assets | 14+11 =25 (8.2) | 4+16 =20 (5.9) | 5+9 =14 (5.3) | 23+36 =59 (6.5) |
| Farm Assets | 16+18 =34 (11.2) | 3+20 =23 (6.8) | 8+14 =22 (8.4) | 27+52 =79 (8.7) |
| **Total** | **165+138 =303 (33.6)** | **171+165 =336 (37.3)** | **114+147 =261 (29.0)** | **450+450 =900 (100.0)** |

Source: Field Study

Each respondent is given three options out of eight items. So the total choices are 300 respondents 'X' 30 options =900 responses. No item can have more than 300 options. As per the above table marriages come first with 189 (21.0) followed by children education 178 (19.9) pucca houses 147 (16.3) and medical care 144 (16.0). In other words the four important requirements are marriages of children, education of the children, pucca houses and medical care and treatment. Farm assets are given 79 (8.7) respondents followed by household assets 59 (6.5), bore well 57 (6.3) and dairy activities are given 47 (5.2) respondents. The requirements given by SCs, BCs and STs are close to a large extent with minor variations. Child marriages and children education are the most important to SC respondents. Children education and pucca houses are the most important to BC respondents. Marriages of children and medical treatment are the most important to ST respondents. In both districts marriages of children followed by children education and pucca houses are the most important requirements in the order of preference. Availability of credit to the respondents for the immediate requirements is examined in the following table.

**Table-3.31. Availability of credit to the respondents for the immediate requirements**

| Caste | Availability | Partly available | Not available | Total |
|---|---|---|---|---|
| BC | 10+7 =17 (36.9) | 15+13 =28 (31.4) | 30+26 =56 (33.9) | 55+46 =101 (33.7) |
| SC | 8+9 =17 (36.9) | 17+16 =33 (37.0) | 32+30 =62 (37.5) | 57+55 =112 (37.3) |
| ST | 7+5 =12 (26.0) | 10+18 =29 (31.4) | 21+26=47 (28.4) | 38+49 =87 (29.0) |
| **Total** | **25+21 =46 (15.3)** | **42+47 =89 (29.7)** | **83+82 =165 (55.0)** | **150+150 =300 (100.0)** |

Source: Field Study

As per the above table 165 (55.0) respondents state that credit is not available. It is natural because these households are already in the midst of indebtedness. Respondents from both districts are near equal in this category of non-availability of credit. 46 (15.3) respondents have credit availability. It implies that only 15.3 per cent of the respondents are in a position to meet immediate requirements by taking loans. Credit is partially available to 89 (29.7) respondents. It implies that 89 respondents can meet one or two requirements but not all the three. The data in the above table shows the inclination of the respondents to borrow further. The researcher while administering the questionnaire has interacted with the respondents and noted down information separately as provided by the respondents. Some of the implications not covered in the tables analysed so far are as follows.

Good numbers of respondents state that their confidence levels are low and feeling of guilty is high for their inability to repay is more. They state that feeling inferior and little hope in future in view of the agricultural prices in the market. Some respondents state that they are susceptible able to vices like alcohol, smoking, gutka chewing and the like to avoid tension and mental unrest. Some respondents prefer loneliness with inhibitions to come into the general public. They feel that the locals and relatives think about their indebtedness always. Some respondents state that their opinions, suggestions and promises are not recognised by others with credibility. Some are easily irritable and find few well-wishers. Majority of the respondents emphatically states that they cannot concentrate more on agriculture and family welfare as the demands of the lenders haunt them. Constant thinking and lack of initiative do not encourage them to take bold decisions. Some state that they are afraid of the lenders to come out into the public. Some aged respondents feel that time alone can solve their problem of indebtedness. IT is also stated by some respondents that the money lenders and commission agents, sometimes, take away the freedom in casting votes during elections by demanding votes to a particular candidate or party.

## Summary

This chapter, like the fourth chapter, is very crucial for this research study. It deals with the utilisation of credit and the implications of rural indebtedness. Rural Indebtedness has been examined in depth and established in the fourth chapter. Rural people have unexpected commitments to which credit is diverted. Utilisation is not effective since these commitments are unproductive. They remain in the vicious circles of poverty and indebtedness from year to year finding no other escape.

Institutional credit is not timely as there are delays. Documentation, middle men approach and terms of repayment are not favourable and as such thy approach the non-institutional agencies accepting to pay higher rates of interest. All these difficulties are given by the respondents in the study. 163 respondents in the study area have taken grain loans on the condition that they should sell produce to the lenders. 65.6 per cent of grain loan borrowers have used the amounts to purchase agricultural inputs. Respondents of Khammam are more in this type of borrowing. ST respondents in both districts of study borrow in more numbers grain loans. Only 120 respondents spend the loan amounts for the purpose they are taken. It implies that there is diversion by 180 (60.0) respondents to unproductive activities mostly. Areas of credit diversion are also analysed and it is noted that health problems, child education, consumption needs and family functions are important areas of diversion. Diversion of credit is more by the respondents of Khammam district and it is mostly by the SC respondents.

Reasons for the year on increase in the overall debt are analysed and it is observed that majority of the respondents offer two or more reasons. Increasing cost of child education, increasing cost of living and mounting expenditure on health problems are the major reasons given. Crop failure is given as a reason by just 11 (3.6) respondents. Cost of child education is an important reason given by Warangal respondents whereas cot of cultivation is an important reason given by Khammam respondents. Sales and purchases of land by the respondents are analysed and it is noted that 32 respondents have purchased land while 18 have sold land. However, 55 respondents are both sellers and purchasers. BC respondents are more in purchase of land and also in both category. Sale of land is more and purchase land also more in Warangal district than in Khammam district. The most important reason for sale of land is to clear of old debts. 26 respondents have sold land for this purpose. Children education and performance of marriages also drive the respondents to sell out land. Respondents (42) in Warangal are more in selling out land when compared to the respondents (31) in Khammam district. Interestingly, 87 respondents have purchased land in the study area and such purchases are from agricultural income saved mostly. 21 respondents have borrowed from non-institutional sources to purchase land. Purchasers of land are also more in Warangal district.

Non-institutional credit component is more in the study area and the non-institutional agencies have occupied the land of 32 respondents admeasuring 71 acres. More SC respondents (15) followed by BC and ST respondents have lost land through occupation. Respondents as well as acres of land occupied are more in Khammam district. Land reforms have benefited 69 respondents with the allotment of 139 acres, and in other words, 231 respondents are not benefited. ST respondents are more (41) followed by SC respondents to benefit from the allotment. Loan moratorium is available to 43 per cent of the respondents. Interest subsidies are available to 24.6 per cent of the respondents. However, 50 respondents have no benefit from the government programmes. Warangal respondents are more in availing benefits from the Government.

Indebtedness affects the overall life of the individuals. Self-confidence comes down and inferiority develops. Status of the borrowers before the lenders and in the locality is estimated. 195 (65.0) respondents state that their status is normal in the society while 172 respondents maintain that their status in the locality is normal. It implies that the status of 105 (35.0) respondents is low before the lender and the status of 57.3 per cent of the respondents is low in the society. More respondents in Warangal district maintain normal status than in Khammam district. BC respondents are less in the low profile category as they are coming up among the weaker sections. Relations of the borrowers with the lenders and local people are also examined. Around 34 per cent of the respondents maintain smooth relations with the lenders and 30 per cent of the respondents with the people in the locality. It implies that rough relations are with 66 per cent of the respondents with the lenders and 70 percent with the people in the locality. Relations are quarrelsome to a large extent with the lenders and locals due to indebtedness. Khammam respondents are more in maintaining smooth relations. SC respondents followed by ST respondents are more in strained relations. Guilty feeling, low confidence level, inferiority complex, frequent irritation and loss of hope, strain relations with the people. Money lenders and private agencies use threats and force to recover loans. 185 (61.6) respondents state that there have been no such occasions. However, 23.3 per cent of the respondents suffer from threats. 15.3 per cent of the respondents have threats rarely. It can be inferred that more than 38 per cent of the respondents face such threats. Threats are limited with regard to BC respondents.

Growing indebtedness disturb the home atmosphere and sometimes family relations may not be cordial. More than half of the respondents fail to maintain cordial relations with the family members. Only 43.6 per cent maintain cordial relations with the family members. 54 per cent of the respondents quarrel with the family members. BC respondents maintain peaceful homes followed by SC and STs. Family life to large extent is influenced by the indebtedness of the individuals.

Problems need suggestions and solutions. This angle of implication is examined by observing in the sharing of the feelings by the respondents. Sharing of the problems gives solace and helps to find out away. 16 per cent of respondents do not share their problem of debt burden with any one. 84 per cent share their feelings with friends and elders in the locality, parents, close relatives, wife and children. Most of respondents prefer sharing with wife and children followed by friends, parents, elders and with close relatives. All the three castes are identical in sharing their problems. Sharing the problem with none respondents are 28 in Khammam against 20 in Warangal. Nature of the suggestions given to the respondents while sharing is examined. 45.2 per cent of respondents state that the suggestions offered are not valuable. It implies that 54.8 per cent of the respondents value suggestions in different degrees. More BC respondents accept that the suggestions are valuable and useful. More respondents in Warangal district feel that the suggestions are not valuable.

Financial assistance from friends, close relatives and social groups is analysed. Indebted people seek help. This aspect of the implications of indebtedness, after analysis is found to be pertinent with 173 respondents only. It implies that 127 respondents have not received any assistance from friends, close relatives and social groups. They have to struggle on their own.

Most of the respondents (40.0) are not aware of the credit delivery and use of force for recovery by the microfinance institutions. 32.6 per cent of the respondents have complete awareness while the remaining have little awareness of the MFIs. This lack of awareness among the rural people is misused by the MFIs.

Growing indebtedness effects the health of the borrowers. 29.3 per cent of the respondents have no health problems implying health problems to 70.7 per cent respondents in different degrees. More BC respondents have no health problems. Health problems are more among the respondents of Khammam district. Health care of the family is influenced by indebtedness as finance becomes a constraint. Less than 1/3rd of the respondents pay attention to the health problems of the family members, implying 2/3rd are not paying attention. Most of the respondents, in view of indebtedness, neglect the health of the family members. Khammam district is slightly better in this aspect. Incidence of depression among the respondents due to indebtedness is analysed. 37.6 respondents have never gone into depression. However, the remaining 62.4 per cent of the respondents suffer from the problems of depression and sometimes become passive, dull and docile. Loss of hope, constant thinking, low self-image and inferiority complex drag them into depression.

Suicide attempts by the respondents/family members in view of the inability to repay loans is examined. 33.6 per cent of the respondents have attempted to commit suicides of which ST respondents are more and BC respondents are less. It is happy to note that $2/3^{rd}$ of the respondents have not been prone to suicides.

Growing indebtedness brings in shift of occupation and this aspect of the implications of indebtedness is analysed only 25.6 per cent of the respondents are positive to shift from agriculture to other occupations. More BC respondents accept this proposition of shift from the occupation. More respondents in Khammam district opt for shift, however, 74.3 per cent of the respondents are not interested to leave agriculture. They are sticky in nature with traditional confidence in land and cultivation. Migration either temporarily or permanently is an implication of indebtedness. Weaker sections in the rural areas migrate to urban centres with a hope to earn and save to repay the old loans. After analysis it is observed that 25.6 per cent of the respondents are willing to migrate to urban centers. More BC respondents are willing to migrate to urban centers in search of jobs. Respondents from Warangal district are more when compared to Khammam district with the desire to migrate.

27.3 per cent of the respondents prefer Crop Holiday to save losses and to stop further borrowing. In their opinion prices of agriculture produce are not remunerative, at least, to cover the cost of cultivation. Surprisingly more ST respondents prefer crop holiday.

Planning by the respondents to overcome indebtedness is examined. Only, 21.3 per cent of the respondents have such plants. Majority of the respondents plan to control wasteful expenditure, then comes generation of more family income by taking up agro allied activities. 52 respondents plan to approach institutional sources to take loans so as to repay old debts.

Expectations of the respondents from the Government in the form of assistance are asked for. Enhancement of subsidies on agricultural inputs, remunerative prices to the agricultural produce and crop insurance, liberal and suitable loan waiver scheme, low rate of interest, development of rural infrastructure and control of inflation are the suggestions offered in the order of preference estimated by respondent counts. The suggestions are close from the respondents in both the districts.

Immediate requirements of the respondents are elicited from out of 8 items giving three options to each respondents. It is observed that marriages come first followed by education of the children, pucca houses, medical care, farm assets, household assets, bore wells and dairy activities. The order of priority is worked out on the basis of respondent counts. In both districts marriages of children, children education and pucca houses are the most important requirements. Only 15.3 per cent of the respondents are in a position to meet the immediate requirements by taking loans. 55 per cent of the respondents state that credit is not available to meet the requirements while 29.7 respondents can get partially. It is observed from this analysis that the respondents, steeped in indebtedness, are eager to look for new credit in view of the pressing needs.

The opinions of the respondents on implications gathered by the researcher during interaction are consolidated at the end of the chapter. Low levels of confidence, guilty feeling, little hope on future, susceptibility to vices, tension, loneliness, inhibition to coming to the public, loss of credibility, irritation, less concentration on agriculture and family welfare, lack of courage and always scared of the demands of the lenders are the implications as given by the respondents. Freedom of the respondents in casting votes during elections is also affected by the non-institutional sources of credit.

The analysis in this chapter validates the third hypothesis of this research study which states "Rural Indebtedness in its implications pervade the overall living conditions of the borrowers, sometimes, posing a threat to the very existence". Implications of indebtedness from different angles are analysed and the consequences of indebtedness from socio-economic, political and domestic spheres of the borrowers are examined. Objectives and connectivities of the study, thus, have guided this chapter.

# 4

# Summary, Conclusions and Suggestions

This research study on "Implications of Rural Indebtedness among the Weaker Sections" has taken two adjoining districts of the Telangana Region of Andhra Pradesh. Three mandals each from Warangal and Khammam districts and two villages from each mandals are selected for the study. 25 respondents from each village comprising 300 respondents are selected as sample for this study. Weaker sections are identified by taking the BC, SC and ST respondents as a criteria. The research work is divided into six chapters with introduction and methodology where in the importance of agriculture and the problem of rural indebtedness besides the research process are given in the first chapter. The second chapter has examined the earlier studies on the research problem to help the researcher with the content, techniques and gaps so as to fit in the findings of this research work into the body of knowledge already accumulated. Profiles of the sample districts, mandals and villages are also given in the second chapter.

As economic activities are the interaction between the physical and human resources socio-economic conditions of the study area are analysed in the third chapter. To examine similarities or otherwise analysis is made separately for each district as they are contiguous. Most of the respondents are below 60 years of age and so age group is in favour of the respondents to face the strain of agriculture. Illiteracy is more and most of the respondents have completed only primary education. Literacy levels among the BCs are more than the other two castes. School drop-outs are more in Warangal district (40) than in Khammam district. School dropouts are less among BC children. Joint families are slowly decreasing as only 1/3rd of the respondents are in the joint families. There are no female respondents from BC households, among the 49 female respondents. Even though housing programs of the Government have provided living accommodation to a great extent 52 respondents still recide in thatched houses. Some respondents take up both agriculture and non-agriculture activities. Medium and big farmers are limited and small and marginal farmers are more in both districts. Absentee landlordism continues in the form of leased lands and dry land under cultivation is in the range of 40-55 per cent. STs are dominant in land ownership in Khammam districts while BCs are dominant in Warangal district. Irrigation facilities are available to some extent and there are variation in the farm size between the two districts. Paddy, cotton and chilies are important crops. There are inter district variations in the cost of cultivation and intra cost variations within a district. ST respondents in both districts have low per acre income from food crops. Inter district variations are noted in the cost of cultivation of commercial crops also. Incomes from commercial crops are more in both the districts. Per acre incomes of the ST respondents are the lowest in the overall study. Efficiency quotients for both food and commercial crops are slightly higher in Warangal districts. Cultivation of commercial crops is noted to be highly remunerative. Average income and average expenditure are higher in Warangal district. ST respondents are in a disadvantage in both the districts. Land ownership is widely distributed. There are similarities in the socio-economic conditions between the two districts.

The basic research problem in all dimensions is analysed in the fourth chapter confining to the hypothesis and objectives. BC respondents are comfortable with higher levels of consumption than the other two castes. There are variations in the consumption pattern between the two districts. More than 50 per cent of the respondents are not able to save because of which they are driven to borrow. BC respondents have more saving potentiality. Non-institutional source are dominant in credit delivery by providing credit to 76.7 per cent of the respondents. The inference is that the institutional sources provide credit to a limited extent which is inadequate. More institutional credit is provided to BC respondents than the other two castes. BC respondents are more in membership of SHGs and co-operatives. Only 47 per cent of ST respondent households have SHG membership. 69 respondents have inherited debts from parents, grandparents and brothers. However, inherited debt is low among ST households.

All the 300 respondents have outstanding debts implying indebtedness across the board. 53.1 per cent of the respondents borrow for unproductive purposes. However, more BC respondents have taken productive loans. Child education and medical treatment account for unproductive credit. Easy availability, prompt delivery, flexible repayment terms, easy approach are all the reasons for non-institutional credit. BC respondents are successful in taking more credit from RRBs, SHGs and co-operatives. SC and ST respondents account for limited institutional credit. RRBs lend more in Khammam district whereas co-operative credit is more in Warangal district. Only one commercial bank, Punjab National Bank provides credit in two villages of the study. Average institutional loan is

Rs. 13,359 and the outstanding due are in the ratio of SC 9: BC 8: ST 7: Money lenders are still important whereas commission agents and relatives and friends are not significant. 192 respondents have taken loans from non-institutional sources and the average outstanding debt is Rs. 22,095. Intensity of indebtedness is analysed and it is found that the average institutional credit due per respondent is Rs. 8270 against the average credit due to non-institutional sources at Rs. 22,095. The ratio of indebtedness caste wise is BCs 35: SCs 31: STs 36:. Interest rates are high and most of the respondents pay between 25-36 per cent as interest. Gold, pass books, phaines are mortgaged, sometimes, to borrow. Loan repayments are irregular and increasing cost of cultivation and unremunerative prices are the reasons attributed. More than 50 per cent of the respondents repay the old loans by taking new loans. It implies that the remaining debt trap from year to year. New debts to clear off old debts are more in Khammam district. Loan waiver scheme has not benefited 53.5 per cent of the respondents even though, all the respondents belong to weaker sections. Quotients indebtedness are worked out to quantify the debt burden in relation to asset values. Overall quotient of indebtedness in the study area is 2.5 implying that the assets are 2.5 times of the outstanding debt. The quotients for BCs, SCs and STs are 3.25-2.5 and 2.04 respectively. STs are in a disadvantageous position and BCs are well placed. Land-debt ratio are also worked out and it is 1:7061 for the study area as whole. It implies that the outstanding due per one acre of land is Rs. 7061. Land-debt ratios are 1:9981 for BCs 1:8796 for SCs and 1:4294 for STs. As land values differ even in a village and from village to village these ratios may not give correct estimation of the debt burden.

The role of institutional and non-institutional sources in the credit flow, debt burden of the respondents, variations in credit distribution from caste to caste, productive and unproductive borrowings are the objectives covered in the fourth chapter. "Incidence of Rural Debt is more among the Weaker Sections with variations" is the first hypothesis of this study and it is found to be valid. The second hypothesis of this study is also verified and it is established that BC respondents have an edge over the other two. It is noted that ST respondents are at the receiving end. Superior status of BCs among the weaker sections is also elaborated from different angles.

Utilisation of credit and the implications of rural indebtedness are analysed in the fifth chapter and so it is very crucial for this research study. Utilisation of credit is not effective and there are diversions of credit to unexpected commitments and unproductive channels. Delay in credit, delivery inadequacy, documentation, middle men and repayment terms of the institutional sources drive the respondents to opt for non-institutional credit even though interest rates are high. More than 50 per cent of the respondents have taken grain loans accepting to sell the produce to the lenders and respondents of Khammam are more in this type of borrowing. There is diversion of credit to meet the expenditure on health care, child education, consumption needs and family functions. It is noted that there are inter district variations in the diversion. Increasing cost of cultivation, cost of living and cost of health care are the major reasons for growing indebtedness. BC respondents are more in the purchase of land. Most important reason for the sale of land is to clear of old debts. Child education and marriages are also reasons for the sale of land. With agricultural surplus. 81 respondents have purchased land. Sale and purchase of land are with in variations between the two districts. 32 respondents are evicted from their land of 71 acres by the money lenders. More SC and ST respondents have lost land through occupation by the money lenders. Land reforms have benefited only 69 respondents with the allotment of 139 acres of land with STs followed by SCs as maximum beneficiaries. Loan moratorium has not benefited 57 per cent of the respondents. Subsidies have not reached 75.4 per cent of the respondents. Government programs have benefited more respondents in Warangal district than Khammam district.

The status of 35 respondents is low before the lenders and status of 57.3 per cent of the respondents is low in the society due to indebtedness. There are inter district variations and inter caste variations in the status profiles. Relations are not smooth with the lenders to a large extent 70 per cent and the relations with the local people are also not smooth as stated by 70 per cent of the respondents SC and ST respondents have strained relations with the locals. There are threats from the money lenders as stated by around 39 per cent of the respondents. Threats are limited with regard to BC respondents. More than half of the respondents fail to maintain cordial relations with the family members and here also more BC respondents maintain peaceful homes. 16 per cent of the respondents do not share their problem of indebtedness with any one and shunned. Most of the other respondents share their problems with wife and children, friends, parents, elders and close relatives. Such sharing is valuable in getting suggestions as stated by 54.8 per cent of the respondents. More respondents in Warangal district state that the suggestions are not valuable when compared to the respondents of Khammam district. 42 per cent of the respondents have not received any financial assistance in case of emergencies from friends, close relatives and social groups in any form. Most of the respondents ($2/3^{rd}$ ) are not aware of the credit delivery and loan recovery methods of microfinance institutions.

Around 71 per cent of the respondents suffer from problems of health due to indebtedness. Health problems due to indebtedness are low among the BC respondents. There are variations between the two districts in the incidence of health problems. Most of the respondents ($2/3^{rd}$) are not in a position to pay proper attention on the health care of the family members and so indebtedness affects the health of the family members. 62.4 per cent of the respondents suffer from the problem of depression and sometimes become passive and dull. $1/3^{rd}$ of the respondents have attempted to commit suicides and among them ST respondents are more and BC respondents are less. $1/4^{th}$ of the respondents are willing to migrate to urban centers. Here also BC respondents are more with in inter district variations. More than $1/4^{th}$ of the respondents prefer crop holiday as the cost of cultivation is more and the market prices are not remunerative. Majority of the respondents plan to control wasteful expenditure and also to generate more family income by taking up non-agricultural activities. Increase in the subsidies on agricultural inputs, remunerative prices, crop insurance liberal loan waiver schemes, low rate of interest, development of rural infrastructure and control of inflation are suggested in the order of preference by the respondents to mitigate the problems of indebtedness. Marriages of children, education of children, and pucca houses are the most important requirements as given by majority of the respondents. However more than half of the respondents maintain that credit is not available to meet the requirements. Only 15.3 percent are in a position to obtain credit to meet the requirements.

This researcher through interactions with the respondents has elicited and recorded the implications of indebtedness separately. Low levels of confidence, guilty consciousness, loss of hope, vices, tension, desire to be lonely, inhibition to coming to the open, loss of credibility, irritation, less concentration on agriculture and family welfare, timidity, constant thinking and even loss of freedom while casting votes are also implications of rural indebtedness.

The third hypothesis of this research study is validated in this chapter. Objectives and connectives as conceived in the first chapter are complied with. Rural Indebtedness is established, analysed in depth and the implications of indebtedness are discussed in detail in the study.

**Conclusions and Suggestions**

1. Most of the respondents are small and marginal farmers. 56.6 per cent of the land in Khammam district and 43.7 per cent of land in Warangal district is dry.
2. Illiteracy is more in the area of study to an extent of 64 per cent. Most of the 36 per cent literates have completed primary education only.
3. School drop-outs in the study area are 19 implying the fact that school age children are out of school.
4. Main occupation of 277 respondents is agriculture while 23 are both agricultural and non-agricultural labour of casual nature.
5. Land leasing and rent payments are observed in both the districts of study indicating absentee land lordism to some extent. There are inequalities in the distribution on land ownership in the study area with STs owning more land in Khammam district whereas BCs owning more land in Warangal district. Average farm size is not

uniform and variations from caste to caste and from crop to crop.

6. Average incomes per acre from commercial crops are more than double to the food crops. Efficiency Quotients for food crops are 1:0.27 in Khammam district against 1:0.31 in Warangal district. At the same time quotient for commercial crops are 1:1.34 in Khammam district against 1:1.65 in Warangal district. Commercial crops are more remunerative than food crops. Efficiency Quotients show the income for an investment of one rupee.
7. ST respondents are in a disadvantageous position with regard to the possession of assets like. Own house, land, bullock carts, tractors, bore wells, TV, two wheelers, cell phones.
8. Institutional sources provide credit to a limited extent and 76.7 per cent of the respondents borrow from non-institutional sources to bridge the gaps in credit needs. Credit delivery to the BC respondents is more since, they are upcoming among the weaker sections.
9. More BC respondents have membership in co-operative credit societies and SHGs. SCs and STs lag beyond in membership of these institutions.
10. All the 300 respondents have outstanding debts, implying indebtedness across the board.
11. 53 per cent of the respondents have borrowed for unproductive activities like medical expenditure and child education. BC respondents are more in taking productive loans.
12. Most of the respondents are not aware of the nature and recovery strings of MFIs.

13. Outstanding credit dues to the institutional agencies are in the ratio of 9:8:7 for SC, BC and ST respondents respectively.

14. Money lenders are very active in the study area by lending to 183 respondents at higher rates of interest. Commission agents and friends and relatives are to a limited extent.

15. Intensity of indebtedness is worked out and the ratio is BCs 35: SCs 31: STs 36. There are variations in the levels of indebtedness. ST respondents are more burdened.

16. Around half of the respondents pay more than 20 per cent annum as rate of interest.

17. More than half of the respondents take new loans to repay the old ones and thus remain in debt trap.

18. Quotients of indebtedness showing the relationship between asset values and outstanding dues are worked out. The overall quotient of indebtedness in the study area is 2.5 and for the BC, SC and STs the quotients are 3.5-2.5 and 2.04 respectively. It implies that the ST respondents have more burden as their asset values are low. Outstanding debt per one acre of land is also worked out in the form of land-debt ratios which are 1:9981 for BCs, 1:8796 for SCs and 1:4294 for STs. Land-debt ratios may not give correct picture of debt burden as there are variations in the value of land within a village not to speak of village to village.

19. Inadequacy of institutional credit and procedural delays in credit delivery by the institutional agencies drive the farmers to hover around non-institutional sources coughing out high rate of interests. Sometimes grain

loans are also taken on the condition of selling the agricultural produce to the lenders.

20. Credit diversion to unproductive activities has taken place to a large extent. Child education, medical treatment, marriages, family functions are the important areas of diversion.
21. Debt burden has been increasing year after year due to increasing cost of child education, cost of living and expenditure on health problems.
22. Private agencies have occupied 71 acres of land of 32 respondents. These 32 respondents suffer from small size of holding and some are converted into agricultural labourers and tenants.
23. Land reforms have not benefited 231 respondents, loan moratorium has not helped 57 per cent of the respondents and interest subsidies are not available to 75 per cent of the respondents.
24. Low status before the lenders and in the society due to indebtedness is considerable. However, more BC respondents enjoy normal status. Relations are not smooth with the lenders, local people due to indebtedness as stated by a good number of respondents. Strained relations are reported by more SC and ST respondents.
25. Credit dues to some extent (38.0). Such threats are limited with regard to BC respondents as they are coming up.
26. More than 54 per cent of the respondents fail to maintain cordial relations with the family members. BC respondents maintain peaceful homes unlike SC and ST

respondents as indebtedness disturbs the farming life and home.

27. Most of the respondents share their problems of indebtedness with wife and children, friends and close relatives. Sometimes valuable suggestions come out from such sharing. Financial assistance from friends, relatives and social groups is to a small extent to the indebted respondents.

28. 70 per cent of respondents suffer from health problems due to indebtedness. Majority of the respondents do not pay attention to the health problems of the family members.

29. 62.4 per cent of the respondents suffer from the problem of depression and become passive and dull. They state that they go on thinking by developing inferiority complex.

30. 1/3rd of the respondents have attempted to commit suicides due to indebtedness. This problem is rocking developed states like Punjab, Haryana and Maharashtra besides some districts of Andhra Pradesh.

31. 1/4th of the respondent want to shift from agriculture to other occupations. More than 1/4th of the respondents are willing to migrate to urban centers in search of a livelihood. This, in turn, many increase the problems of urban centers due to congestion.

32. Control of wasteful expenditure, generation of more family income and approaching institutional sources to take new loans to repay old debts are accepted as solutions by a majority of the respondents as being planned.

33. Enhancement of subsidies on agricultural inputs, remunerative prices and crop insurance, loan waiver scheme, development of rural infrastructure and control of inflation are the expectations of the respondents from the Government under policy measures.
34. Majority of the respondents state that marriages of children, children education and pucca houses are immediate requirements. But only 15.3 per cent of the respondents are in a position to meet them.
35. Low confidence level, less concentration on agriculture, negligence of family, tension, irritation, loss of credibility, lack of courage, affective the personal, domestic, social, lives of the respondents due to indebtedness. Sometimes private lenders may coerce, the political options of the indebted rural folk during elections.

## Suggestions

1. Illiteracy is the root cause for all the evils in civil societies. Illiteracy can be wiped out by encouraging adult education and in this effort the help from NSS, NCC and NGOs be taken by the Government at the gross root level. Promotion of literacy is the panacea for all the problems of the rural societies.
2. School drop-outs are to be controlled to ensure, at least, minimum education. Reasons for drop-out be analysed and such children be induced to join schools again. Incentives like free uniforms, midday meals be introduced to attract the drop-outs.
3. Dry land is more in the districts of study. Most of the farmers are of small and marginal categories. Hence,

irrigation facilities be extended and crops suitable to the dry lands be identified through research as such problem cripples the country as a whole.

4. Incomes from commercial crops are more than the incomes from food crops. This may lead to food crisis if farmers are inclined to allocate more land to commercial crops. Food security is very vital to a country like India. Remunerative prices to the produce and incentives to the food crop growers go a long way to stem the tide.
5. Co-operative societies, SHG linkages help the farmers to get loans at low rates of interest. SC and ST farmers be encouraged to become members by creating awareness. Then only weaker sections can get the benefit of low interest rate.
6. Awareness about microfinance institutions be created to discourage borrowing. They exploit the innocence and ignorance of rural people and use force to recover loans. Loans from the money lenders are also to be discouraged.
7. Rates of interest charged from the farmers be controlled by the Government. Legislative measures to cheek the rate of interest be initiated on farm loans.
8. Inadequacy of institutional credit be checked. Procedures and documents be simplified. Timely credit be provided by the institutional agencies to the farmers.
9. Unproductive activities like child education, medical treatment, marriages, family functions eat away the loans taken and so alternative arrangements be made. Institutional agencies may be encouraged to provide credit for unproductive activities to some extent.

Educational loans by banks be made more liberal and easy. In states like Punjab, group marriages to minimize expenditure are encouraged. Rural India needs such arrangements to reduce expenditure on marriages.

10. Corporate bodies have made child education and medical treatment very costly, especially in Andhra Pradesh. Government schools should be developed to attract more children. Government hospitals be provided with doctors, medicines and paramedical staff to reduce the expenditure on health related problems by the rural people.
11. Private agencies have occupied by force the land of some farmers as observed in the study area. Legislative measures be initiated to protect small and marginal farmers. A few states in India have already introduced legislative measures to protect the marginal and small farmers from losing land.
12. Moratorium and interest subsidies be extended to more number of weaker sections. In 1975, the then Prime Minster Smt. Indira Gandhi took a bold decision to declare moratorium even on private loans in the old 20 point economic program. Strong political will is needed to initiate such measures.
13. Counseling by village phanchayath, SHG group leaders, NGOs and Panchayaths from time to time be provided to the indebted farmers. Their mental balance is to be restored. Their human dealings be improved through guidance and counseling.
14. Medical checkups from time to time be arranged in the rural areas by the health department. Service organisations like lions, Rotarians should be involved in

such camps. They suggest medicines and drive out the incidence of depression. Institutions like co-operative societies, SHGs, teacher associations better hold small meetings to prevent suicides. They should convenience the debtors that if not today tomorrow the loan can be repaid. Life is more important than loan repayment. Counseling helps to tackle their problems also.

15. Occupational shift and migration to urban centers are twin implications of indebtedness. By developing agro based industries, household industries, diary, poultry, piggery, sericulture, sheep raring and the like income generation can be increased in the rural areas. Along with agricultural income sources of income in the agro allied activities discourage shift and migration.
16. Control of wasteful expenditure and sticking to the traditional norm to "Live within means" should be the watch ward not only in rural India but also in urban India. Counseling in this direction be provided.
17. Institutional sources need to come to the rescue of the indebted farmers by providing a onetime loan to clear off private loans.
18. Central and State Governments in their policy measures should consider more subsidies on agricultural inputs to reduce the cost of cultivation. Remunerative price mechanism and minimum support price to guarantee incomes be taken up. Crop insurance and loan waiver scheme be widened to cover more small and marginal farmers. Development of rural infrastructure is imperative to make marketing easy and remunerative in rural areas. Above all, control of inflation is a must to

reduce the cost of living. Then only loans for consumption come down.

19. Government housing programs to weaker sections should be extended more to cover wide range of households of the weaker sections.

20. *Swaminathan Commission* has given suggestions on Farmers' Distress (2004-2006) to achieve the goal of "faster and more inclusive growth" as envisaged in the Approach 11th Five Year Plan. It follows:

    - Enhancing productivity, profitability, and sustainability of the major farming systems of the country.
    - Policy reforms to substantially increase flow of rural credit to all farmers.
    - Special programs for dry land farming for farmers in the arid and semi-arid regions, as well as for farmers in hilly and coastal areas.
    - Enhancing the quality and fast competitiveness of farm commodities so as to make them globally competitive.
    - Protecting farmers from imports when international crisis fall sharply.
    - Increase water supply through rain water harvesting and recharge of the aquifer for should become mandatory.
    - "Millions wells recharge" program, specially targeted at private wells should be launched.
    - Substantial increase in investment irrigation sector under the 11th Five Year Plan apportioned between

large surface water systems, minor irrigation and new schemes for ground water recharge.

- Expand the outreach of the formal credit system to reach the really poor and needy.
- Reduce rate of interest for crop loans to 4 per cent simple, with Government support.
- Establish and agriculture risk fund to provide relief to farmers in the aftermath of successive natural calamities.
- Issue Kisan Credit Cards to women farmers, with joint Pattas as collateral.
- Develop an integrated credit-cum-crop-livestock-human health insurance package.
- Expand crop insurance cover to cover the entire country and all crops, with reduce premiums and create a Rural Insurance Development Fund to take up development work for spreading rural insurance.
- Implement a universal public distribution system. The commission pointed out that the total subsidy required for this would be 1 per cent of the Gross Domestic Product.
- Help small and marginal farmers to improve the productivity, quality and profitability of farm enterprises and organise a Rural Non-Farm Livelihood Initiative.
- Restructure of Microfinance policies to serve as livelihood finance, i.e. credit coupled with support services in the areas of technology, management and markets.

- Public awareness campaigns to make people identify early science of suicidal behavioral.
- Improvement in implementation of minimum Support Price (MSP). Arrangements for MSP need to be put in place for crops other than paddy and wheat. Also, millets and other nutritious cereals should be permanently included in the PDS.
- MSP should be at least 50% more than the weighted average cost of production.
- Encourage Non-Farm employment opportunities by developing particular sectors and sub-sectors where demanded for the product or services is growing namely: i) trade, ii) restaurant and hotels, iii) transport, iv) construction v) repairs and vi) certain services.

Ever since, independence much has been said about agriculture and farming community. Policy measures by the Central and State Governments have been attuned to develop the cultivators and change the rural scenario. But from time to time problems change and change is the order. Until and unless the Indian farmers feel confident with all happiness, Indian economy cannot be on firm foundations. Rural Indebtedness is to be checked to in fuse such confidence in the farming community. A strong agriculture provides a strong base not only to rural India but also to the nation. Gandhiji dream of self-sufficient, Grama Swaraj can be realised on that day. Till then, let us all wait and hope.

# Bibliography


B.N. Hiremath Professor Theme Paper "The changing faces of rural livelihoods in India" *Institute of Rural Management*, Source: NADEL-ETH, SDC –p 3 2007 (adapted).

Dr. R.K. Panda, "Agricultural Indebtedness and Institutional Finance", Ashish Publishing House, Punjabi Bagh, New Delhi, 1983, pp 120-123.

Dr. Y.D. Pujari, "Rural Indebtedness: Causes and Consequences" *Indian Streams Research Journal,* Vo. 01 Issue 01, February, 2011 PP. 124-127. Dept. of Economics, D.B.F Dayanand College of Arts & Science, Solapur.

Ghatak Shambhu, 2007. *A Case for Indian Agriculture.* http://topics.developmentgateway.org/poverty/rc/ItemDetail.1117760?itemId=111770 (Accessed on October 28, 2007)

Government of India (2005), Situation Assessment Survey of Farmers-Indebtedness of Farmer Households, NSS 59th Round (January-December 2003), Ministry of Statistics and Programme Implementation.

Gurumeet Singh, "Revitalise Agriculture through Rural Credit", *Financing Agriculture-A National Journal of Agriculture & Rural Development,* September-October, 2008, pp 3-4.

Hiremath B. N., K. V. Raju and Anil Patel (2004). "Farmers' Technology Adoption, Farm Management and Livelihood System Gujarat". In "*In Search of Sustainable Livelihoods: Managing Resources and Change"*, Ruedi Baumgartnet and Ruedi Hogger (Editors), pp. 94-125, Sage Publications, New Reserve Bank of India Bulletin, May 1999.

Indian Economy: Source:www.iloveindia.com/economy-of-india/agriculture-india.html

Jayasheela and Vishwanatha, "Agricultural Credit in the Post WTO Period,"*Agricultural Situation in India*, January 2008, 1467 Agri/2008 – 4, pp 485-489.

K. Kareemulla*, "Bank Credit for Agriculture versus Farm Indebtedness in Uttar Pradesh", *Agriculture Situations in India.* January, 2008. p 472.

Mitra. MK; Roy. DC and Mishra. SK, "Rural Indebtedness: Concept, Correlates and Consequences: A Study of Four Tribal Villages in the North Lakhimpur subdivision, Assam" *North-Eastern Hill University, Shillong,* online at http://mpra.ub.uni-muenchen.de MPRA Paper No 1824, Posted 07, November 2007.

Narayanamurthy, "A Study of the Net incomes of Farm Households in the state of Punjab, NSSO

NSSO (2005). Indebtedness farmer households-situation assessment survey of farmers NSS, 59th round. Report # 498 (59/33/1) Ministry of Statistics and Programmed Implementation. Govt. of India. Pp26.

Parimal., V. Rao, "New Insights into the Debates on Rural Indebtedness in 19th Century Deccan", *Economic & Political Weekly*, January 24, 2009, pp 55-61.

PERI (1997) A Study of the Semi Formal Financial Institutions:Co-operative Credit, Punjab Economic Research Institute, Lahore.

Praduman Kumar, Mruthyunjaya, Madan M Dey Long-term Changes in Indian Food Basket and Nutrition, Economic and Political Weekly September 1, 2007, pp: 3567 3572.

S. Gandhimathi and N. Sumathi, "Availability and Distibutional Disparity of Agricultural Credit, Financing Agriculture" – *A National Journal of Agriculture & Rural Development*, September-October, 2008, pp 12- 17.

Sainath, P, 2006. *Politics of Packages & the Packaging of Politics: Indian Prime Minister Faces the Dead Farmer Problem*, July 21, 2006.

Sainath, P. *It's the Policy, stupid, not implementation, India Together*, Sun 28 Oct 2007. http://www.counterpunch.org/sainath07212006.html. accessed on October 28.

Wolff, H., *Co-operation in India*, Thacker Spink and Co., London, 1927, p. 3.)

www.business.mapsofindia.com/sectors/agriculture.html

www.business.mapsofindia.com/sectors/agriculture.html

www.iloveindia.com/economy-of-india/agriculture-india.html

www.iloveindia.com/economy-of-india/agriculture-india.html

# Index